MW00724124

HOW ASIAN WOMEN LEAD

Lessons for Global Corporations

Jane Horan

palgrave
macmillan

First published in 2014 by
PALGRAVE MACMILLAN®
in the United States—a division of St. Martin's Press LLC,
175 Fifth Avenue, New York, NY 10010.

Where this book is distributed in the UK, Europe and the rest of the world,
this is by Palgrave Macmillan, a division of Macmillan Publishers Limited,
registered in England, company number 785998, of Houndmills,
Basingstoke, Hampshire RG21 6XS.

Palgrave Macmillan is the global academic imprint of the above companies
and has companies and representatives throughout the world.

Palgrave® and Macmillan® are registered trademarks in the United States,
the United Kingdom, Europe and other countries.

ISBN: 978–1–137–37871–2

Library of Congress Cataloging-in-Publication Data

Horan, Jane.
    How Asian women lead : lessons for global corporations /
Jane Horan, EdD.
        pages cm
    Includes bibliographical references and index.
    ISBN 978–1–137–37871–2 (hardback)
        1. Women executives—Asia—Case studies. 2. Leadership in women—
Asia—Case studies. 3. Leadership—Cross-cultural studies. I. Title.

HD6054.4.A78H67 2013
658.4′092082095—dc23   2013025822

A catalogue record of the book is available from the British Library.

Design by Newgen Knowledge Works (P) Ltd., Chennai, India.

First edition: January 2014

10 9 8 7 6 5 4 3 2 1

Printed in the United States of America.

CONTENTS

PROLOGUE: SETTING THE STAGE FOR THIS BOOK

My journey toward understanding the styles of Asian women's leadership began in a luxurious penthouse office of a multinational chief executive. The high-rise office building was sandwiched between Hong Kong's Fragrant Harbor and the Happy Valley Race Course, and a heated phone conversation was taking place.

It was at the beginning of the Chinese New Year holiday, and red envelopes (*hóngbāo*) stuffed with money were being given and received across the SAR (Special Administrative Region) of eight million people, living cheek-by-jowl in a space the size of Manhattan. The symbols and rituals during the Lunar New Year place tremendous importance on three values which underpin the success of one of the most capitalistic cities: money, spirituality, and family, in that order. It was the time of year when many organizations also see an exodus of staff, once corporate bonuses are paid (assuming the gods of good fortune smile on everyone). Everyone was on holiday except for a female executive I will call Mitchy.

"She what?" the CEO screamed into the phone, as I sat in one of the soft leather chairs next to his desk, listening to one side of the story.

"No," he trailed off.

"Can't believe it." A note of insincerity has crept into his voice.

Then he made an unprintable comment that translated to "Good riddance."

He hung up and turned to me: "Mitchy quit." There was a tone of relief in his voice.

I knew immediately what had happened. Mitchy, born in Taiwan and raised in London, was an executive vice president who had been hired by our company three years ago now a corporate star. She had turned around a failing business, weeded out weak performers, and created a solid five-year business strategy for our Asia division. She had, however, just been forced out. Six months earlier she was on the fast track headed for a bigger role at the global head office in New York. But there were concerns about her leadership style. She pushed herself very hard to succeed, always on a level with the global CEO, and demanded the same pace from her team. At times she was emotionally overwrought, other times very direct, with a blunt, unapologetic style. Yet she was a strategic thinker and visionary leader, attributes in short supply within our company. Culturally, we were a "nice" corporation, light on candid feedback unless it was positive, and the corporate culture had an indirect, less confrontational style of communication.

Mitchy, however, was different. She delivered frank feedback, challenged the status quo, and poked many sacred corporate cows, including our trusted consumer brand and corporate policies. Precisely because of her prodding style, she turned the business around quickly, restoring profitability and goodwill. The leaders of the organization liked what they saw in her bottom-line results but could not warm up to the messenger. Mitchy's strengths in the battle ultimately became weaknesses when she started negotiating her next position.

What happened to Mitchy is a textbook case of relying too heavily on a few competencies and overemphasizing certain strengths. Eichinger, Lombardo, and McCall believe an overemphasis on one strength derails many global executives (McCall 1998; Lombardo and Eichinger 1989 and 2006; Kaiser 2009). Some organizational consultants highlight the power of strengths while others focus on the dangers of overemphasizing a single skill rather than using a repertoire of leadership competencies (Kaiser 2009). Organizations, situations, and people change. The skills that almost assure success in one culture may be ineffective elsewhere. Mitchy's candid conversational approach and direct questioning of systems chafed against the culture at corporate headquarters. Her strategic ability and take-no-prisoners style served her well in emerging markets, but it was beyond the threshold of acceptance with executives in North America. In studying success factors of global leaders, researchers found that "strength in one culture could become a decided disadvantage in a different one" (Kaiser 2009, 48); Mitchy is one example of an executive's overreliance on a skill or strength, which eventually blocks the person's upward trajectory to the next level.

At that time I was the Asia Pacific Organizational Development Director for the corporation and knew this was Mitchy's "last dance"; there would be no further coaching, no careful, constructive feedback leading her further up the ladder. Ironically, she was pushed out by the person who hired her, an alpha male with a rather overbearing ego. She didn't stand a chance. Neither did others who followed in her footsteps. The pendulum had swung. Mitchy's replacement was the exact opposite; an overly detailed planner, the new hire was reluctant to challenge the status quo. But she too failed despite using an alternate style. I have seen variations of this incident played out in my 20 plus years of working with multinational corporations in Asia, overseeing organizational development, talent management, leadership development, and cultural integration. Part of my role was succession planning, developing the strategy to create future generations of leaders in Asia. Mitchy's story was not an isolated incident; yet, the stories of women leaders I have worked with, despite the similarities, are not merely variations on a theme. Each one has led me to conduct the research on leadership which I present in this study and to reflect on individual leadership stories in various categories, industries, and cultures. I have no single conclusion but have uncovered success stories and insights throughout the lives of four Asian women leaders.

ACKNOWLEDGMENTS

I would like to acknowledge and thank the following without whose help the dissertation from which this book developed would not have been possible.

To Dr. Sheila Trahar, my sincere appreciation for providing tremendous support, continuous guidance, tireless patience, and valuable insights and wisdom throughout my learning journey and the writing process.

To my trusted literary advisor, John Willig, thank you for belief in this project and continuous support.

To the wonderful Palgrave Macmillan team: Leila Campoli, Kristy Lilas, and Sarah Lawrence for timely guidance and support.

To my participants, who will remain nameless, my thanks for providing time, energy, and life stories.

To my family Neal, Hank, and Elah: thank you for your boundless patience, endless support, and ongoing encouragement.

CHAPTER 1

A Road Map for the Book

This chapter provides the groundwork for the book, and gives reasons for the study. The prologue provides a snapshot of my experiences as head of organizational development in multinational organizations. I have seen this story—talented individuals falling off the leadership ladder—many times and have often pondered why this happens. After years in the corporate world, I returned to graduate school to obtain a doctorate in leadership education. Three serendipitous events spurred me to pursue this path of study and use the mechanism of narrative inquiry or what is more commonly known as storytelling.

The first event was my reading of a captivating research paper on multicultural narrative inquiry by JoAnn Phillion (2002). Her story and imaginative writing intrigued me. I found this use of narrative provided a powerful method to learn about multicultural environments. Second was a paper on ethical leadership and finding connections to women and transformational leadership (Eagly 2007; Ciulla 2004). The third event was the chance meeting with Ms. Lim, a

Malaysian Chinese businesswoman and mother of three teenage boys. Ms. Lim was born into a prominent family and attended prestigious boarding schools; she was never the best student and only aspired to become a flight attendant. She now runs a successful global hedge fund. Hedge funds are among the more demanding areas of investment banking, and only a few women are at the helm of such funds. Ms. Lim's story, coupled with my experiences in developing and facilitating leadership inside organizations, aroused my curiosity. I wanted to understand how women—particularly Asian women—navigated the road to leadership. These events sparked my interest in cross-cultural narrative and my desire to learn about leadership from women in an Asian context.

In this study, I use narrative to explore the complexities of life and leadership experiences of four women in Asia, each immersed in the intricacies of culture, particularly within an organization. Asia, with over 3.3 billion people, provides enormous growth opportunities and will continue to be at the top of the population charts for the foreseeable future. Digging into the demographics, we find highly educated women now entering the workforce in droves and organizations struggling to maintain diverse and inclusive leadership (Hewlett 2007). The demographic and economic shifts in Asia predict positive developments for the region while simultaneously presenting demands on organizations and leadership. As headlines continue to highlight the dearth of women in leadership positions, the research on women leaders (specifically Asian women) remains sparse. Accordingly, this cross-cultural narrative inquiry provides a new perspective for both organizations and for qualitative research.

Interestingly, women enter the workforce at the same rate as men, but their numbers noticeably diminish as they move up the organization (Aguirre and Sabbagh 2010; Coffman et al. 2010; Barsh et al. 2012). There are many reasons for this: demands of work and family, vagaries in talent selection, organizational politics (Barsh and Yee 2011; Hewlett 2007), to name a few. The focus of my research is to gain insight into leadership from the experience of women in academia and nonprofits and from women entrepreneurs and businesswomen. Understandably, there are many ways to gather data. Since this research explores the human side of leadership and organizational life, narrative is well suited to this study. I use the terms narrative, narrative inquiry, and stories throughout this book. Stories provide suitable conditions for understanding and expressing the human experience of events, choices, and leadership (Polkinghorne 1995). From this perspective, I examine four women's leadership experiences in Asia.

A single theory should not hold authority over another, and while there is much quantitative research on leadership, this study uses words rather than numbers as data; stories provide a different perspective on leadership and culture. From a postmodernist perspective, stories evolve, as do interpretations. This study looked at multiple perspectives, including my own, in order to guide the interpretive process. The fluid nature of narrative allows interpretation to evolve, holding back from a definite view. Stories regenerate with each reading, and each time are interpreted through different prisms and perspectives.

In the process of doing this research, I reconsidered my Western thought process and my deeply held beliefs about Asian culture, both during interviews and in my subsequent writing. This presented opportunities, conflicting emotions, and learning. At times I connected with my participants, and at other times I was left baffled, unable to make any meaningful connection. From my first interview I struggled with the meaning of words and the participant's response. This may sound amusing but is true. Simple words used every day offer new ways to understand culture and organizational systems. My challenges often came from holding on to a particular meaning, relying on the same ideals and structure by which I was in fact also challenging the participant (Derrida 1978). Conducting cross-cultural interviews unearthed mistaken beliefs and exposed misinterpretations inherent in both Western and Eastern cultures.

Struggle can both educate and elucidate. In writing about leadership and culture, there are no absolute truths, but rather different ways to examine assumptions about truths. Similarly, as will be discussed in chapter 8, there are few definite definitions of leadership; the prevailing definitions reflect a Western perspective. Leadership—like science—should not be considered unilaterally or from a dominant cultural perspective. The complexity and diversity of global business and society distort our view and certainly should challenge a universal understanding of leadership. I do not intend to offer vague solutions or uncover truths about leadership and demonstrate specific steps to get to the top. Instead, I focus on and explore values, influences, and experiences from a combined perspective on how these women *experienced* leadership. This research is collaborative, based on the journey of women at multiple junctions of life. I am an integral part of this story traveling alongside my participants. This qualitative method explores the past, sometimes from a historical perspective, sometimes from a current perspective, sometimes from a cultural one, all to gain insights and create meaning based on multicultural views. In the end, this book highlights various viewpoints for understanding an underrepresented community of leaders.

Cross-Cultural Storytelling

Narrative allows multiple interpretations for many people. These stories provide lessons of experience and serendipitous moments of realization on the road to leadership. A story is never straightforward, and a challenge immediately exists. Context, situations, and the fluid nature of stories can unnerve, be endlessly creative, or be perpetually interpreted (Denzin and Lincoln 2005). Learning takes place through a reflexive process. Reflexivity looks both internally and externally for answers. A story presents itself one way, but going back and reading it again provides another angle, multiple interpretations and ways to tell a story. Some of these stories start with the interview sequence, others begin from a different angle, and all blend culture and historical elements. Each story presents a window into the participant's self, leadership, and culture providing a representation of life for the reader's interpretation.

As previously mentioned, the decision to use cross-cultural narrative began with my interest in JoAnn Phillion's (2002) research on narrative multiculturalism. However, my exposure to qualitative research and using stories began at university with Erving Goffman's book *The Presentation of Self in Everyday Life* (1959), which laid the groundwork for narrative performance. Unlike Phillion, I entered this research without a prepared script. Phillion carried "scripts of expectation" into the Bay Street school, stating "the truths of the script were what I personally and professionally believed in and tried to practice" (2002, 268). In my research, I deliberately did not have a script but unconsciously carried baggage of cultural knowledge and mental frameworks into this narrative. I also uncovered bias, a gut reaction to a story or thought that prevented me from accepting a new perspective. This experience provided much learning and profound insights on what happens inside organizations for women. In chapter 7, bias is explored in more detail with links to culture, gender, and invisible barriers for women in organizations.

My background in cross-cultural development should have eliminated such bias, but I had to remind myself (constantly) to look at the corporate world and these women through a very different lens. I left the United States over 25 years ago to study Chinese language, history, and culture in Changsha, Hunan Province, in China. Under the leadership of Deng Xiao Ping, China was then a very different country from today. In 1985 summer indicated tomatoes or watermelons and few other varieties of food. I taught English to graduate student engineers at one of the large mining and metallurgy universities. The university resembled a small city with 100,000 or more residents living within the walled enclave. My fellow students wore Mao suits, studied the *Little Red Book* on Saturday afternoons, and few spoke English. I later moved to Hong Kong and was employed by a Shanghainese family-run company; subsequently, I worked in multinational organizations across Asia for over two decades. Through these experiences and my own personal development, I became sensitive to Asian cultural values and was made painfully aware of the increasing demands on women at work. Using cross-cultural narrative inquiry to engage and collaborate with my participants provided insights into culture and undoubtedly more questions.

Leadership Research and Storytelling

Stories have been used as a research method in education and leadership for years (Clandinin and Connelly 1990; Ciulla 2004; Helgesen 1995; Brown and Rhodes 2005; Howard 2010). As I was writing these stories, a thought or picture of a past event would fleetingly enter my mind, and I carefully tried to capture these thoughts. Taking a step back, I recognized similar events with my participants—events or moments in time when decisions were made to shift, change, transform, or step into leadership. More important, these short-lived moments provided valuable learning about leadership and self, but only through reflection. Recognizing these events—moments of realization—during the interview process, I started to see similar events appearing in each story. These events were not tragic—indeed, many are delightful (the offer of a new position or business opportunity)—but often linked with pain or emotional upheaval. Reading these stories, readers will find many such turning points in each.

Stories are performance art. Sitting in a trendy Hong Kong café or a wood-paneled Singapore office, pictures unfolded in my mind while listening. Many times I thought I had seen this movie before. I was aware that bias entered my thoughts. Returning to my notes provided a new perspective to make sense of the scenes unfolding. The words now carried a different meaning. Looking back, I have questioned and doubted the interview process, wondering if the stories represent my participants' voices. But how do we accurately represent a voice and grab a memory? As the story retreats, it floats between center stage and back stage.

Moments of Realization Defined

During interviews and story writing, moments of realization precipitated periods of reflexive analysis of the process of narrative inquiry and my unchecked bias (Finlay 2006). These pivotal moments became apparent as I was writing the stories and seeking my participants' reflections. One participant responded, "You know me better than I know myself."

These moments of realization, either spontaneous or over time, defined a time when participants realized the need to change course, when there was not a choice, and when leadership was thrust upon them. These moments were critical junctures for me with my participants and within the stories. Listening to their stories, I experienced many of these moments and remembered my time in the corporate world, on the other side of talent meetings, observing and advising leaders.

There were many occasions when I was headed in one research direction but forced to take a step back, and in doing so, I learned something new. The word "failure" provided significant learning from a personal and organizational perspective. In chapter 9 the misinterpretation of words is discussed in greater detail together with its impact on leadership and organizations. The setback with words (specifically the word "failure") forced a review of these stories and leadership. As I was doing so, these serendipitous moments of realization emerged. These epiphanies happened suddenly when a thought, statement, or story triggered a memory. Or they came slowly when a belief was accepted, challenged, or disregarded. Such reflexive moments illustrate the tremendous importance of noticing a specific response in order to make a predictive action (Etherington 2004).

In chapters 2 through 5, such moments are highlighted in each story. Throughout this study, I lived within my participants' world and experienced episodes of discontinuity with narrative inquiry and multicultural environments. In chapter 9 multicultural mishaps are discussed in more detail, exploring definitions of culture and identity and their impact on organizations. Some of this confusion stems from using a Western concept of leadership and accepting cultural stereotypes. Using reflexivity in this study helped me assign meaning to popular myths surrounding leadership. Instead of seeking truth or generalized perspectives, the stories are intended to build awareness and cultivate interest in future leadership in a global context.

Participants in This Study

The women in my research discuss family, spirituality, and personal attitudes toward leadership. Their families play an integral role, weaving an interesting dynamic throughout. Setbacks abound—either losing a parent early in life or rejecting a parent in adulthood and reuniting with parents in midlife—and these women attribute their success to family support and to integrating work and personal life.

I am fortunate to have lived in Asia and developed an extended network in business, academia, and nonprofits. I am also a member of many women's networks and have held two board positions for nonprofit organizations. Embarking on this study, I reached out to this extended network, provided an overview of my research, and asked for introductions to women in leadership positions. I was not seeking to interview CEOs or managing directors but was more interested in one or two levels below. I wanted someone who was on a path of leadership, leading a function, department, or nonprofit, and I planned to broaden the scope of this discovery beyond the business community.

My only criteria were diversity and time. I wanted diversity in culture and experiences—participants had to be willing to spend a year or more of many interviews and story iterations. I received a few responses from prominent business leaders and many from European and American women with extensive experience and impressive credentials in Asia. I decided against both, as business leaders could not afford the time and I was focused on stories of Asian women. I soon started the interview process of over 30 women in the region. The interviews and research required time and commitment, and I was honored that my participants chose to be part of this journey with me.

I have not worked with or for any of them; none are colleagues. But I was introduced to each one and decided to invite them to take part in my research. I intended to write stories across the countries in Asia but received wise advice that this might not be feasible. I started with six stories and whittled this number down to four. I wanted to maintain diversity of cultures, experience, profession, seniority levels, and industry. The four women I selected represented "success," and could identify and articulate the foundation of their success. Yet, theirs is not success in a conspicuous sense of achievement—financial, for example, accompanied by fame and fortune. In fact, reframing success to honor their cultures, these women believe their achievements are the result of having been offered opportunities, having had a commitment to learning, and having taken the time for self-reflection. From my vantage point and in my words, these women are "successful in more ways than one."

In keeping with the narrative form, I had a broad set of questions I intended to ask, but I also maintained flexibility to allow each individual story to flow. I used my plan as a guide, not a strict format. When participants asked me to send the questionnaire in advance, I realized I needed to provide an overview of narrative, how the process works, and a road map of the journey. I was aware of the cultural aspects and saw that this guide was important because some participants required an overview before our first meeting in order to prepare. In addition, the guide aided in building rapport and trust. The overview outlined the process and broad areas to be discussed; it highlighted confidentiality, disguising names or industry, and other connections. My intention was to engage in a general dialogue to understand various experiences relating to leadership and life. Mindful of the ethical aspects of this study, the overview provided a general guideline without being too prescriptive (Josselson 2007).

To conduct the interviews I used a digital tape recorder, but there were many times when this device failed. Hence, most of my interviews were with a journal or sometimes both a journal and a recording device. I prefer to write, as it allows me to jot down thoughts or memories in side columns. At the end of the interview, I would reread my notes and add comments. When writing the interview, I waited for the story to unfold. I sent back the original transcripts to ensure I had captured what the participants meant to say and asked for corrections or clarification of any misunderstandings. During our meetings, the conversations were never straightforward, moving in different directions, often veering off in new areas. When I interviewed Ms. Ali (see page 12), for example, we went back and forth many times, as one question or correction would lead to another topic. After completion, I sent the stories to all the participants. I waited and waited for a response. I nudged and reminded them on many occasions of the impending deadline. Some did not respond until I was almost finished with the manuscript. One participant corrected a few lines and asked me to change the segment on identity. For another, her story brought back memories of a difficult transition representing a different frame of mind although she now has a changed perspective on life. The comment adds to the complexity of stories and life, reinforcing the temporal nature of both. Julian Barnes, acclaimed author and recent Booker prize winner, considers the same thoughts, "The past is a distant, receding coastline, and we are all in the same boat" (Barnes 1984, 110). Together we were in the same boat, creating stories that sometimes sting with truth, but from a distance often bring a less harsh view.

Examining the careers and lives of four successful Asian women, I uncovered their success through hard work, serendipitous events, and sheer determination to work through visible and invisible barriers. Their setbacks were described as "moments of realization" that propelled them forward, even when their support systems gave little support and they were faced with a challenge or opportunity. When the ground seemed to fall away under their feet, they pressed on regardless, to achieve balance, harmony, and success in a hierarchical, monetary, and spiritual sense.

The stories invite the reader to navigate the ever-changing nature of human events and lived experiences. While the stories are open to interpretation and to explore multiple leadership perspectives, I have used transformational leadership as a foundation for this research. There are two reasons for drawing on the knowledge of transformational leadership research. The first is the morally grounded, ethical stance of transformational leadership (Ciulla 2004). The second reason is the connection to women (Eagly 2007). I have not tested my participants on this style, but consider this thinking as a basis of understanding. Throughout this study I refer to transformational leadership, Sally Helgesen's (1995) narrative on ways women lead, Cheung and Halpern's cross-cultural narratives on women executives, and McKinsey's centered leadership model, all discussed in greater detail in chapter 8.

Influences of Feminist Ethnography

Ethnography (not necessarily feminist) encompasses anthropology, education, sociology, and cultural studies (Skeggs 2001) and is "grounded in the particularities of women's lives and stories" (Behar and Gordon 1995, 15). A woman interviewing women leaders in a male-dominated environment (Chin et al. 2007) is analogous to female ethnographers finding themselves "within a discipline rooted in male musings about foreign lands" (Behar and Gordon 1995, 2). Living in Asia, I immersed myself in the cultures of these women. We travelled, lived, and worked in the same places. The similarity of experience was the impetus for exploring feminist ethnography. I believed the stories of women leaders were not always readily available or discussed. The work of Ruth Behar, Deborah Gordon, Kamala Visweswaran, and Stacilee Ford is relevant from a cross-cultural and feminist perspective. Gender, culture, and experience do not have one-size-fits-all solutions, so gathering insights from a variety of sources made sense. Narrative inquiry provided a platform for exploring and experiencing the social and organizational world of these women and allowed for many voices to be heard (Richardson and St. Pierre 2005). I learned how these different perspectives come together and offer additional perspectives on these stories.

Meaning and Sense Making

My intention has been to learn and share learning about leadership from these women: the richness, the complexities, and twists and turns along the journey of leadership in Asia (Etherington 2004). This cross-cultural inquiry—unbeknownst to me—originated in college, was further enhanced by my work, and was complemented by my living outside of my home country; it was motivated by watching talented women being overlooked for leadership positions. I began and ended this research sensitized to my position by the women who participated in it. I am one of them, with no positional power over them, but on a par with them (or one level below) in terms of their achievements. They are not world-famous, nor will we see them in magazines or on television, but they are leaders in their own right, at work, in their communities, and at home. The narratives allowed their voices to be heard and their personal experiences and events to illustrate leadership from their perspective. That I was part of this community and lived in their cultures benefitted this research and the emerging leadership stories.

To analyze these narratives I use the entire story or multiple stories, looking at each one individually and collectively to evaluate this research. The story provides the context for life choices and unfolding leadership. The moments of realization are turning points, either disruptive life events or unforeseen opportunities, requiring a choice between doing nothing and moving forward. Whatever the decision or course of action, all the stories provide meaning. While words often were hurdles, making sense of this data comes from the entire story. I amassed data, and some words were excluded because not every detail is needed to tell a story (Polkinghorne 1995).

While I struggled with content and representation, I also grappled with what to include. These stories include interview notes, historical references, leadership research, cultural insights, and personal reflections. I struggled with how to adequately represent my participants. Their stories provide one view, but I wanted the reader to see multiple perspectives. In chapter 6 I use narrative fiction to bring my participants together to discuss workplace politics and organizational dynamics. Using a fictional voice on a typical organizational dilemma through the eyes of my participants offers another view of these women.

How this Book Unfolds

I have come to know my participants on a deeper level in the course of the years of research through corresponding with them regularly to check details, clarify observations, and gain more insights into their paths toward leadership. They are not my friends but very close acquaintances. At the beginning of my research, I assured them all that their names would not be revealed, as some are identifiable in Asia. To ensure anonymity, their identities are disguised. It is my desire to remain faithful to these four, who are, in nom de plume, Ms. Ali, a Bangladeshi academic, Ms. Ito, a Japanese social entrepreneur, Ms. Chin, a Singaporean executive, and Ms. Lee, a Taiwanese executive. I hope their insights will challenge the reader to reflect and grow. Using a qualitative approach, the following questions emerged:

> How do women experience leadership and how do values, choices, influences, and family all converge and impact on each of their stories?
>
> How does narrative inquiry contribute to the understanding of gender and leadership in a multicultural landscape?
>
> How does the combination of narrative and reflexivity provide guidance in narrative across cultures and with unconscious bias?

This study evolves through the stories to uncover the human side of leadership. The first part of the book consists of individual stories; the second half explores leadership and multicultural theory to uncover their applicability to organizations. Following a postmodernist perspective and allowing freedom within the chosen framework, I use an unorthodox approach, beginning with the women's narratives in the first four chapters. I purposely place Ms. Ito and Ms. Ali together under the category of moral leadership. The subsequent stories of Ms. Chin and Ms. Lee are concerned with the "how" of leadership—how to build a connected, inclusive web for success. The final chapter focuses on leadership for the future, looking back in order to move forward, asking the bigger question: "what does all this mean?"

I encourage the reader to experience and engage in these stories as part of the "performance." As I listened to my participants, a comment would sometimes take me back to my memories, of my own "moments of realization," memories of where I had come from and where I had travelled. My participants' words stay with me as a writer, fellow traveler, cross-cultural, female ethnographer (Denzin 1997; Richardson 1994). Each story provides a different narrative angle, the pieces fitting into the puzzle of leadership for the future. With this in mind, it is my hope that the reader has similar moments of realization.

Moral Leadership

Three passions, simple but overwhelmingly strong, have governed my life; the longing for love, the search for knowledge, and an unbearable pity for the suffering of mankind.

These passions, like the great winds, have blown me hither and thither, in a wayward course, over a deep ocean of anguish, reaching to the very verge of despair. . . .

This is what I sought, and though it might seem too good for human life, this is what—at last—I have found.

Bertrand Russell *(Russell 1975, 9)*

CHAPTER 2

Akiko Ito's Story: Life Is a Game

That everyday should be a fiesta seemed like a marvelous discovery

Ernest Hemingway

Akiko Ito is an architect and organic food chef by training, a leader of a nonprofit business by desire. Raised in Japan, she spent most of her formative educational years just outside of Tokyo. She left Japan for the first time at the age of 18 on a school trip to Europe while studying architecture. She left again at 20 to study English in Canada and later travelled to Central and South America to study Spanish. Once back in Japan, she moved to the small village of Miyoshi in Chiba Prefecture, where she lived in a collective farming commune to study organic farming. She left Japan for good at age 24, going to India, Nepal, and other Asian countries for a year before settling in New Zealand to launch a successful organic fast food company. Travelling to different cultures provided Ms. Ito with an incredible knowledge and insightful learning about herself and her role in different communities. Her leadership and work are based on the value of giving, transforming the way business works today. She created and now leads a nonprofit organization to make possible easy access to global giving, ensuring medium to large enterprises achieve corporate social responsibility objectives.

I interviewed Ms. Ito in the summer of 2009 and have kept in touch with her over the years, going back and forth with this research and in the process learning more about her endeavors. As with all good stories, let me set the stage for how I came to know Ms. Ito. Late in 2008, I was asked to interview Somaly Mam for a women's conference in Singapore. Sold into slavery at the age of nine, she now runs a foundation in Cambodia to help other victims. A formidable leader, Ms. Mam is listed as one of the 100 most influential women in the world by *Time* magazine. I had originally intended to interview Ms. Mam for this book, yet scheduling time and geographic distances made it next to impossible to carry this out. I wanted to uncover learning from those we may seldom hear or see mentioned in the media, the unsung leader doing essential work in business, community, and society.

At the end of the event and after interviewing Ms. Mam, I shared a taxi with a young woman entrepreneur and mentioned my research on Asian women leaders. She said, "You must meet Ms. Ito, who leads a nonprofit organization focused on driving sustainable change one step at a time." Listening to this short synopsis, I wanted to hear more. Like many Asian women leaders, Ms. Ito travels frequently, and finding a time to meet was challenging. In the summer of 2009, our schedules connected, as we were in Singapore at the same time. I met Ms. Ito at a small café overlooking Clarke Quay. Ms. Ito looks young, small with a quiet smile; you could walk past her and not realize she is in the room until she starts talking, and then you are captivated.

Difficult Times, Early Influences

As a young girl growing up in Japan, Ms. Ito experienced relentless violence and chaos at home and school. Relationships were tightly controlled at home and at school, where she was often disciplined with sticks. She grew up in a dysfunctional family; her father was an alcoholic who was cruel to her mother. Her mother was a conformist and enabler for these incidents. The prevailing attitude, Ms. Ito commented, was that "there were rules to follow, and you were punished if you didn't follow them." Her mother followed the rules of the house, the formality, and tradition of family hierarchy. The wife's role is tethered to and supportive of upheavals in husband's career. Traditional roles and presentation of self in society follows strict rituals and protocols which are uncommon outside of Japan. Following Confucian hierarchy, women are raised to respect older male family members. For mothers this focus means the son will achieve educational success by entering the right schools (Lebra 1998). Social and traditional pressures ensure this ranking is maintained and that order is kept intact (Winfield et al. 2000; Buruma 1991)

Life for Ms. Ito and her mother under such rules was challenging. A chaotic environment also prevailed at school. Ms Ito shared this story, "I found primary school scary. I was constantly afraid of being judged. My teachers didn't like me. I was afraid to go to school and afraid to talk. I remember bringing a caterpillar home and telling my mother, 'This is my best friend.' My mother was visibly upset. Growing up in Japan, I was different."

To be different in Japan is not necessarily a positive attribute. This seemingly innocent statement, "my best friend is a caterpillar," not only raised eyebrows in Japanese society but created a genuine concern from the collective conforming society. Recalling this story reminded Ms. Ito of an old adage, "A protruding stake must be driven into the ground" (Winfield et al. 2000, 331). She was not beaten down, but those experiences provided the basis for who she is today: "I do what I do now because I don't want to hurt anyone." She said, "I am here to give value. Nothing is scary anymore."

Today Ms. Ito leads a global nongovernmental organization (NGO) connecting business and nonprofit organizations to drive sustainable change and make a difference toward eradicating poverty and hunger, an idea she thought of while watching poor children play on the streets in India, and Central and South America. She travels globally, conducting business via email, iPad, and iPhone. A single mother of two, she uses technology to keep her connected and balanced. In her mid thirties, petite and quiet, she commands the attention of executives, government officials, and academics. She uses vivid stories and speaks with authority, connecting with her audience through the voice of experience and authenticity. From this small profile comes powerful speech, an authentic, caring nature that rings out loud. Juxtapose this with her life a few years earlier when she was terrified of talking in front of a group. "Before any speaking engagement my hands would sweat, my voice would crack, and I'd often burst into tears." With a purposeful mission and practice she overcame a difficult past, and her fears.

A Wayward Traveler

She left Japan in her early twenties with a rugged backpack that insulated her from pain. "I didn't want family and didn't want anyone," she said. "I wanted to pursue learning and creativity. I went to Europe after obtaining a professional certificate in architecture. I was inspired by the people, language, and the buildings." Reflecting on her travels, she thought, "This is different. I drifted. I had no plans." Ms. Ito travelled to Canada to learn English. For two years she lived with families, but she never really opened up, partly because she didn't have command of the language and felt uncomfortable sharing her heart or speaking about her experiences. "I lost my words and couldn't speak properly, so I used children's language. I felt good using children's language; it was simple, authentic, and real." She described living in Canada as "like a dream, where everything was new, where I started a new life after losing everything." She had been closed but was opened up: "I let go of stuff, including my childhood. My newfound happiness came from rejecting everything."

Travelling through developed and developing countries provided the groundwork for the "social entrepreneur" work she now does. The idea to help others came from her life experiences and what she witnessed travelling. "I watched school children on the dusty streets of India, with little food and clothing, running around, smiling, and laughing. They had so little but were so happy. I just remember marveling at them." "I believe that when we give, we feel abundant, and when we're not giving, we feel we don't have enough, and that others have more. Everywhere I went I saw this—people giving and sharing are the happiest, and they are surrounded by others who are loving. I found this to be particularly true in my travels to Guatemala and Costa Rica where I went to learn a little Spanish."

Fiesta Begins, Philosophy Unfolds

It was in Guatemala that Ms. Ito had her life-changing experience. Standing on a street corner with her backpack on, she watched as people stood in line for a bus. She felt a desire to get on a bus and travel anywhere, no destination in mind. So she climbed on that bus, no specific destination in mind. As the bus travelled along the dirt road, she checked her backpack and realized her valuables had been stolen. Everything. Money, passport, and credit cards were all gone.

"Suddenly I realized that life was just a game," she explained. "This was the first time I started to play with the idea that life is a game, and that feeling has stayed with me. I said to myself 'OK, let's see how this plays out'. I was not scared, but mostly intrigued by the situation." Now forced to rely on her own resources and instinct, she felt strangely safe. Five hours later, she decided on a whim to get off the bus at a tiny village called Santa Rosa. She had no explanation for getting off at this point, only that the name sounded like a saint's name, reminding her of something from childhood. The streets were empty. With little command of Spanish, she started knocking on doors and explaining with hand gestures that she had no money, but could cook and clean. No one responded to the little Japanese woman. She recalled, "Most looked at me like I was crazy." One woman offered a room. "I stayed for a couple of days, cooking and cleaning. The woman had very little, two small children and no place for me to stay. But she was kind and offered a place on the floor of her children's room. I remember staring out the window, writing in a journal, admiring the serenity of the place. Yes, I knew I had to do something, but at this moment I was happy with my surroundings and playing the game."

"This was crazy and not something I would do again," she added. "This was a very exciting time in my life. I was not a tourist in a big hotel. I just kept playing the game and enjoyed the fun. I remember asking myself, how can I maximize this game?" Looking out the window one morning, she saw a familiar symbol, a truck with a red cross. Ms. Ito realized she could alert the international aid agency of her situation, and so she did. She explained, "The Red Cross brought me to the Japanese embassy." Sitting in the stark quarters, opposite the grey metal desks, the shrill of Japanese ringing in her ears, she noticed what looked to her to be the sullen faces of her countrymen. As she recalled, "The embassy staff was so cold, and they kept telling me I was silly." She continued, "One of the senior staff members who looked very wealthy didn't want to help." As a matter of fact, she said, "Everyone at the embassy looked wealthy, but they refused to help." She recalled, "I was sitting in the office watching everyone caught up in paperwork, procedures, and bureaucracy." To her, they seemed lifeless and completely rigid. Comparing the village and embassy, the contrasts struck her. "The villagers who had very little were more willing to help than the wealthy expatriates on the embassy team. The consular general looking down at me asked, 'What were you thinking, you silly girl? Where are your parents?'"

"Watching his lips move, I thought, 'They are the last people I would call.'" Ms. Ito told me, "My parents didn't know I was in Central America, and I wasn't going to call them. I never give too many details to them. I travel where I want to go freely. I sat quietly on the cheap folding chair outside the senior minister's office observing the all-too-familiar rituals of respect. I knew this is not where I wanted to be. So, I got up and walked out. Down the street, I met another group of travelers and kept travelling. Eventually, I made it home." The development of Ms. Ito's mind-set did not end in South America. She continued using the game philosophy, travelling wherever the mood took her. Travel gave her a sense of freedom and allowed her to be unencumbered by life's demands.

Bucolic, Enlightening Adventure

Returning to Japan, she lived on a collective organic farm near Hokkaido. This farm was very different from the Japan she knew. In the village, farmers lived a simple existence, helping one another. One farm would grow corn and another potatoes. As winter set in, each person chipped in to help the other. "I had never experienced anything like this," she said. "I felt at ease in this village, no pretense, no rules, no hierarchy." This experience in Hokkaido propelled her to learn more about food and organic farming. She went to New Zealand to learn about organic farms and cooking, then to India to learn Ayurvedic medicine, then on to Nepal and Thailand. "It was in India where I had the idea to help others, and a *'feed the world'* concept started to emerge." Returning to New Zealand, she started a fast-food organic food business with very little money and rapidly built it into a chain of outlets with 150 distributors. Ms. Ito recalled, "My idea was to build soup kitchens in India to feed the poor. I was too busy with this business and had no time to do what I wanted to do—give back."

After moving to Australia, she developed blisters on her hands and was unable to work properly as a cook: "I was driving down the road, and I looked at my hands and started to cry. I cried and cried and cried. I realized I wasn't seeing the most important thing. The message was not that my hands were stopping me from cooking, but they were giving me time to pause and figure out that the most important thing was not the cooking. The message was clear; my role is to help others." Even while she was dealing with this unknown disease, the game philosophy reinforced her approach to question each difficult or puzzling situation. On that drive, she stopped the car, looked at her hands, and asked, "What are you trying to teach me?" The realization about her blistered hands brought healing. It was not about pushing herself. It was about letting go. She moved away from restaurants and into the work she does today, transactional giving. Transactional giving allows small and medium enterprises as well as individuals to redirect revenue to specific projects or groups to make a difference in the world. For example, a chain of restaurants gives a percentage of revenue and a section of its restaurants for at-risk adolescents to study and offers tutoring to help them stay in school. The restaurant gives a monthly percentage of its revenue to a group of qualified tutors, and free restaurant space is offered to both students and tutors. Her organization provides the same platform for this type of giving. Her business is now a foundation operating across Asia and expanding globally. "Now things are simple and easy. Life is easy because it is just a game. Lessons happen every day because I don't live for a big reason. My goal is to live to be caring and open. Things happen continuously to remind me to be present and to be the best I can possibly be—not the external me but the internal me." Ms. Ito lives life by one motto: "Enjoy the game at the maximum level." She follows this philosophy completely. While building the NGO an idea popped into her head to write a book. Busy with two children and her business, she took a few days off to write a book. Taking a couple of days off, she sat down and wrote a self-help, motivational book sold widely at independent, spiritual book shops. The book is a self-published one, a short, enlightening publication about living life intentionally and positively.

A Moment of Realization

The first moment of realization, when her philosophy of life unraveled, occurred on the bus to Santa Rosa. Without identification, money, and only a slight command of Spanish, she turned inward and perfected her "life is a game" philosophy. Looking out the back window of the bus, where the exhaust pipe coughed and dust swirled, Ms. Ito thought of the game and relaxed. She simply drifted along for a few hours on the bus and waited for a sign to get off. The game philosophy was refined during this trip, and since remained as her guiding force. Not only has her philosophy provided a calming influence in otherwise terrifying moments, but it has also provided her with powerful insights into life, culture, and spirituality.

As she sat in the chair at the Japanese embassy in Guatemala, she noticed the difference between two cultures. The Japanese culture she thought she understood, and the Latin American culture she was beginning to understand. Comparing the wealthy Japanese expatriate staff with the poor residents in Santa Rosa provided clear insights into the differences between modern societies and developing nations. Comparing the two cultures, she saw people with the least gave the most, and those with much more gave little. This connection and reflection is the basis for her business in transactional giving. Reflecting on that journey, she said: "It turned out to be the most enjoyable, life-changing trip."

The second moment of realization for Ms. Ito's future business came from her experience with the collective farming community in Chiba Prefecture, a five-hour drive from her family home in Tokyo. Japanese cooperative farming dates back to the 1950s, but the movement took hold in the early 1960s when farmers opposed to resort developments and golf courses united in a new movement of social justice (Moen 1992, 1997). Ms. Ito was not aware of this movement until she came upon this collective community. She stayed one year, learning about farming and the values of co-partnerships, or *teikei*. These collective communities were extremely diverse and included academics, agricultural scientists, medical doctors, journalists, and farmers, all involved in various facets of the organic farming movement. She also discovered that particular communal farm had previously been written off by the Japanese government as infertile, and scheduled to be turned into a golf course with high-priced condominiums. However, peaceful resistance from the farmers in the collective had saved the land; they made it fertile and turned it into a prosperous organic farm.

Ms. Ito observed and learned about risk-sharing, bartering, and the extensive varieties of organic vegetables. The community worked as one. If a snowstorm wiped out a crop, they offered assistance, either with another crop for bartering or with an entire meal to share. In addition to meals, the community developed and maintained the watering systems, using mountain water for the rice fields. Although the plots were small, the meals were large, each farmer contributing one item and everyone joining together to eat. Ms. Ito had never experienced this style of collective living and giving before in Japan. The learning from this time raised her awareness and interest in organic farming and bartering for the common good.

Her third moment of realization was having the debilitating hand disease; it caused her to look inward, which ultimately determined and guided her purpose. Ms. Ito believed cooking was a way to serve others and recalled the utter devastation and subsequent depression of not being able to cook. Ms. Ito reenacted the hand movement as she retold the story of the drive on the dusty roads of Australia's backcountry. The story was depicted with such raw emotion that for those few moments I believed I was in the car with her when it happened. There is an emotive quality to Ms. Ito's real-life adventure story, which is offset by her physical presence of wide-eyed wonderment, gentle smile, and calm demeanor. Interviewing Ms. Ito and hearing her story and attitude toward life reminded me of Eckhart Tolle, a spiritual teacher and author of *The Power of Now* (1999). Coincidentally, when I asked Ms. Ito what books influenced her, she responded, *"The Power of Now"*; the book was on the *New York Times* best-seller list and is a spiritual manifesto on consciousness, enlightenment, transformation, and self-awareness focused on living life in the present.

My Moment of Realization

As I listened to Ms. Ito's story about Central America, I recalled my travels in China in 1985. On one occasion I stood at the bus terminal in Beidaihe, a beautiful beach town where Mao Zedong and Deng Xiao Ping vacationed. I walked out of the station into the crossroads of 20 bus drivers honking, waving, and shouting in a language I did not know. Like Ms. Ito, I travelled through the country with little money, a cursory knowledge of the language, and few concerns about where I was going. I stood on the dusty street corner and looked around amidst the cacophony of sounds. Most of the people stared at me; others shoved, pushed, giggled, and spat. Everything was unfamiliar: sights, sounds, and smells. I thought about what to do, how I was going to get to where I wanted to go, and wondered if I should get back on the train to Beijing. Like Ms. Ito, I had set out without anyone knowing where I was, including me. I started to laugh. It was not a game but more like a comedy.

Physically and culturally we were different. Yet, her adventurous spirit and desire to help others are the same as mine. While I do not have the same "life is a game" outlook, I admire Ms. Ito's philosophy and find strong links between this value and entrepreneurial leadership. Ms. Ito sees connections and patterns and uses this knowledge to create something new. More than being creative, she is also concerned about the greater good and making a difference in the world. In her words, she "dreamed of the business I am now doing, connecting people, business, and giving. I did not do this alone; there were plenty of people who helped me get where I am today." The humble quality of Ms. Ito's leadership rings true here.

Ms. Ito places little value on material goods and has a real sense of what leadership for the greater good means. She is globally aware, empathetic, authentic, and acutely cognizant of the future needs of this world. In my opinion, such authentic quality is in short supply and desperately needed in a world marked by greed and financial misappropriations. This authenticity links with Ms. Ito's continuous study of self, her moral compass, which aligns harmoniously with internal values and her external being (Kellerman and Rhode 2007). Ms. Ito lives in harmony with her values, true to herself through the work she chooses to do and her impact on others. In every interview with her, I asked about values through early influences. A telling anecdote was that in response to my question of early influences, she quickly replied "No one!" When I questioned this further, Ms. Ito affirmed that neither her parents nor teachers had any influence on her. In fact, it was the *rejection* of this authoritarian rule and strictness of Japanese culture that led her to break away. Renouncing familial and cultural values put Ms. Ito on a path of self-discovery and mindfulness, that is, being aware of self, others, and the surrounding community. Self-awareness is the first step in mindfulness and leadership (Coughlin et al. 2005; McKee et al. 2006). Reflecting on Ms. Ito's journey, I would posit that the road to her self-awareness provided deep insights on self and community. The "game" philosophy gave Ms. Ito the mental space to become an observer of life and recognize the subtle nuances and revelations in each event in order to move forward, change plans, and chart her course. Each event caused Ms. Ito to reflect and ask, "What is the situation trying to tell me?" Consciously, she looked for hidden meanings in external events, a reflexive process more than internal meditation. Reflexivity is the ability to reflect on experiences to uncover new meaning and respond differently in the context of a continually changing environment (Etherington 2004).

Living outside of Japan and distancing herself from the rituals and values, she still retained some ceremonial traditions. During the first few months of starting her business, things unraveled, events were not running smoothly, and the business teetered on the edge of collapse. "I fired myself as a leader in front of my team," she recalled. Taking responsibility for the problems, she called a meeting, moving to the center of the stage she began with a deep ceremonial bow and announced she was stepping down. In Japanese fashion, Ms. Ito used the painfully deep *saikeiri* bow to represent her dishonor, show respect, and offer apologies to her team. The significance of both bowing and knowing the right bow is considered a fine art in Japan (Buruma 1984), and its importance should not be underestimated. After the tsunami in Japan when the Fukushima reactors failed in

2011, Masataka Shimizu, president of Tokyo Electric, was ridiculed for the short duration and angle of his bow. His use of a 90-degree angle versus a deep 45-degree bow was viewed as indicating that he was not sincere (Walker 2011). After Ms. Ito's public apology, she indicated, "The team achieved some very important break-throughs." She believes that "without this action, we would not be where we are today." This humble quality, placing her team before herself, came through on many occasions. When I asked her to tell me about leading this business, she deferred to her team, indicating the team members were responsible for the success. This statement can be attributed to growing up in a collectivist society. This self-effacing quality is vastly different from an individualistic cultural value of self-promotion, visibility, and talking about achievements. Despite world travels, leaving family, and resisting cultural norms, Ms. Ito's cultural origins ring through in each interview. Modern Japan has not changed nor have Ms. Ito's beliefs; she follows tradition in placing group demands before personal desires.

Following her moral compass, Ms. Ito built a business of help-ing others through transactional giving. There is much discussion on transformational leaders focusing on bigger issues of social and community concerns and operating beyond profit and loss and bal-anced budgets (Ciulla 2004; Eagly 2007). Moral values remain at "the heart of transforming leadership, which seeks fundamental changes in society" (Ciulla 2004, x). These values have the power to change thinking and become transformational when put into action (Ciulla 2004). Assuming this premise of moral values and transfor-mational leadership are valid, we can notice links not only with Asia, but also with Confucianism (Spence 1990; Fairbank 1992; Bass and Steidlmeier 2004).

Concluding Thoughts

As I take a step back to think on my time with Ms. Ito and consider the tenets of transformational leadership style, I find that through her business she not only lifted her team but the business community as a whole by partnering for the greater good of humanity. Moving away from the restaurant business, she created a global nonprofit with the sole intent of making the world a better place. Her leadership and commercial philosophy is based on similar transformational principles: (a) the moral character of the leader, (b) the ethical legitimacy of values embedded in the leader's vision, articulation, and program which followers embrace or reject, and (c) the morality of the processes of social ethical choice and action that both leaders and followers engage in and collectively pursue (Bass and Steidlmeier 2004, 175). While I did not interview members of Ms. Ito's team, I am familiar with the team of dedicated volunteers tangentially connected to her business. Ms. Ito embodies many qualities of transformational leaders; she is morally grounded, bases her actions on her values, and is authentic (Bass and Steidlmeier 2004; Kouzes and Posner 2002). Her life has been full of self-discovery, community concern, and with a high regard for followers, she remains grounded in integrity. With each curve encountered, she managed to turn obstacles into positive change. An outlier most of her life, she always remained true to herself. Her internal concerns and external actions are inextricably linked. In creating her business, Ms. Ito had a simple, yet compelling vision for the future, "to make an impact and leave the world a better place."

CHAPTER 3

Faria Ali's Story: Live Well, Love Well

There is no greater agony than bearing an untold story inside you.

Maya Angelou

Ms. Ali is a young emerging leader with a PhD in sociology from York University in Toronto, Canada; she teaches leadership to young women from the Middle East and South Asia. Ms. Ali was born in Bangladesh, moved to Thailand during her formative years, and attended university in Canada. A global citizen, she is comfortable working in many cultures. She is an academic motivated by learning and the desire to make the world a better place through knowledge. Ms. Ali's story moves from chaos to confusion; early on, she rejected Islam, culture, and country but embraced all three in adulthood. Through her intellectual and personal journey of awareness, she explores Islamic leadership inside and outside Bangladesh. Reading through the research on transformational leadership (Ciulla 2004), I found strong links between

Ms. Ali's philosophy and transformational leadership focused on the greater good.

I had been invited to join an international symposium in Bangladesh sponsored by Prime Minister Sheikh Hasina and the former first lady of Britain, Cherie Blair. Foreign dignitaries, academic leaders, and politicians from the Middle East, Asia, the United States, and the United Kingdom were in attendance, and the focus was on educating the next generation of women leaders. Originally, I had intended to interview a senior female politician in the Bangladeshi government, but she was unable (or perhaps unwilling) to be part of this study. The university provided names of women in leadership positions who might be interested and have time to participate. Ms. Ali was one of those named, and when we met, I asked if she would like to be part of my research. She agreed, and I interviewed Ms. Ali in Bangladesh in January 2011, and we continued regular correspondence and discussions via email until late 2012.

Sheik Hasina opened the conference with 300 women attending with, *"As-Salamu Alaykum"* (peace be upon you). This customary Islamic greeting was in tandem with security forces sweeping for bombs on the other side of the conference room doors. Listening to the opening remarks, Ms. Ali turned to me, saying, "There is no such thing as peace here." She was correct. As we entered the hallway, we moved through a dilapidated X-ray machine, a flimsy, makeshift curtain separating men and women. A young security guard dressed in khaki-green fatigues, army boots, and a vibrant, colorful purdah and sporting bright pink lipstick waved a small, handheld scanner over us. Ms. Ali was dressed in a muted green silk sari with matching subtle jewels and made her way toward the entrance. Together we climbed the steps and stood back to appraise the room and find a place to sit. The air conditioners, old and musty, roared as they pumped out cool air, interrupted by constant electrical surges. Pungent smells of onions, curries, and sweet perfumes permeated the hallway. University students, foreign dignitaries, and the media representatives were cordoned off to one side, a few feet from the stage. There were no windows. The stage, empty and dark, stood silent with red velvet curtains casting a somber hue over the beginning of the Women's Conference in Dhaka City. Outside the conference hall, young women in national dress stood in a long line, waiting patiently to catch a glimpse of the foreign dignitaries.

Bangladesh has a history of political unrest and widespread violence (Rashiduzzaman 1994; Talukder 1975). Born into political upheaval, Ms. Ali originally intended to study Bangladesh's history of acrimony, instability, and culture on the road to democracy. Along with strife and political bloodshed, the country also endured years of flooding and famine. Geographically, Bangladesh is well positioned for natural disasters. Should a cyclone similar to the one in 2007 hit again, the entire country could sink into a watery grave. Each year heavy rains flood the Ganges, and over 5,000 people die annually (Hanley 2005). After more than forty years of separation from Pakistan, the country remains in chaotic transition. Ms. Ali confided, "I never thought of returning to Bangladesh, but I am here and for the first time in years reunited with my parents." It was the sense of adventure and a call to teach leadership that brought her back. A sociologist by training with a keen interest in the Muslim diaspora, Ms. Ali now teaches leadership to young women. The road that led her here has been filled with contradictions and upheavals.

A Tumultuous Beginning

For 36 hours in 1971, six-year-old Faria Ali sat with her little sister in the dark hallway of her home in Dhaka, East Pakistan, as violence swept her city in the fight for freedom. The Pakistani army was cracking down on unrest in East Pakistan for the last time. With India's help, East Pakistan would soon become the independent nation of Bangladesh. But on that day people were dying. Faria whispered to her little sister not to be afraid as she heard students in the street nearby shouting:

> *Ebarer shongram, muktir shongram, ebarer shongram, shadhinotar shongram* . . . this time the revolution is for freedom, this time the revolution is for liberation. (Bhatti 2011)

There was no sign of her father. Her mother paced the floor. Eventually the girls drifted off to sleep. Faria woke up to hear her mother shouting to her father. "I don't care where you find a job, but we're not living here." They soon managed to get out and moved to Thailand, leaving Bangladesh and its violent road toward independence. In Thailand, Faria's father found a teaching job, and the girls attended a Catholic international school with students from South Asia and South East Asia. Ms. Ali said, "It was not the most expensive international school but private nevertheless." Ms. Ali and her sister arrived early for class in a small public bus from the outskirts of town, the only two Bangladeshis in the school. The student body included scions of wealthy families (she recalls one boy who received a Mercedes-Benz sports car for his birthday), a few students on scholarships, and the children of some of the teachers.

The Ali family never displayed outward signs of affluence, and compared with others they were not wealthy. "It felt good to wear a uniform—I never liked free dress day," Ms. Ali, now 36, recalled in our interview. In a life characterized by contradictions, she preferred order and structure. Contradictions began early in life; her mother came from an aristocratic family and married an idealist. Her father worked three jobs to pay for his schooling. Deeply involved with the socialist movement, he walked around the house quoting loudly from Karl Marx. After moving to Thailand, they returned to Bangladesh every summer, and the disparity and contradictions were still evident. In the morning the driver dropped them off for high tea at their mother's family compound, and in the evenings they hailed a rickshaw to return to the slums for a meal with her father's family. Her father had seven brothers and a sister. Only two of the boys went to university. Her father has a PhD, and her uncle became a doctor. Her parents had a strong sense of social service. Her mother's motto was: "If you are noble, you should give to others." These values laid the foundation for Ms. Ali's career choice and leadership style.

Identity Questions

Ms. Ali still continues to struggle with identity: "When people ask, 'Where are you from?' I cannot give a simple answer. My parents grew up in Bangladesh when it was still part of Pakistan. I was born in Bangladesh, spent 12 years in Thailand, and then moved to Toronto to attend university. If I say I am from Thailand, they reply, 'But you don't look Thai.' If they continue to question me, I answer, 'I am from all of these places, but not from any one place. I am part of many worlds.'" "Part of many worlds" is a fitting description for Ms. Ali, as she has adapted to many cultures. Pondering that comment, she briefly considered identifying herself based on her religious view, but then quickly added, "I am more spiritual than religious. Spirituality is important to me, but not religiosity; it is less about belonging to a community of common beliefs and more about belief, faith, and love for the universe and life. Religions offer a wonderful way to connect with forces larger than us and see beauty. My parents were not religious. We knew we were Muslims but did not grow up with Islam."

Her battles with Islamic identity began early in life. She recalls working on a school project in Thailand with a group of Hindu Indian classmates; she was not aware of the differences (between India and Bangladesh) and focused solely on finishing the project. She was out sick for two days, and upon her return was told that she was no longer part of the group. "They said, 'Your people are killing our people.' In their eyes, I was a Muslim." Soon after, she turned her back on Islam.

"I did not want to be Muslim. My views of Islam were tainted by these remarks at the ongoing strife. I was worried that if I looked too deeply into Islam, I would not find a positive side. My classmates and the media's constant barrage of negativity about Islam reinforced this fear. I wanted to dearly hold on to the idea that all religions had a common universal message. But I was scared that Islam would prove me wrong. My defensive and naive reaction was to distance myself from it."

These challenges continued at university. "I was forced once again to face unanswered questions about Islam," she said. She was at university on 9/11, and after the attack on the World Trade Center, the mood in the streets of Toronto was tense. "I remember the day was crisp and cool, not a cloud in the sky. Steam bubbled up from the manholes as my boyfriend and I walked arm in arm down the sidewalk. In the distance, we saw a college friend coming toward us. He barreled into my boyfriend, pulled him close, reached around his neck, drew a knife, and shouted, 'You Muslim lover!' The anger was so intense." Looking back, she blinked and realizes everything could have disappeared. The feelings and questions around Islam returned. "This time, instead of running away, I wanted to understand what it meant to be a Muslim." Ms. Ali became resilient and turned inward. This was a pivotal moment in her life and a driving force in her evolving understanding of what it means to be Muslim impacting the work she does today.

Early Influences and Turning Points

Early influences in Ms. Ali's life were her mother, teachers, and books. She drew energy from books and read voraciously, encouraged by a mother who instilled in her a love of learning. The American authors, Alice Walker, Maya Angelou, and Toni Morrison left lasting impressions. "I identified with these authors on gender, violence, and identity. I also liked Victorian writers; these writers dealt with family aristocrats and poor families, something I was examining in my own life." Coincidentally, the Victorian writers link with the puritanical aspects of Bangladeshi culture, specifically the purdah or veil and the related requirement for women to wear a scarf and other restrictions on women and their roles in society (Sultana et al. 2009). Ms. Ali's family did not follow these rigid rules, but elements of traditional values remained. In primary school, she explained, "I failed a test and my mother was furious. My stubborn streak came out. Turning inward I said to myself, 'I will show her.'" By showing her mother, she discovered a love for mathematics. Gifted in math and chemistry, Ms. Ali received a scholarship to medical school, which she subsequently declined.

Graduate school provided a time for her to reflect on learning and life. She discovered Charles Tilly, a sociologist and prolific writer from Columbia University. "Any time I am stuck, I pick up one of the many texts by Tilly. I cannot pinpoint exactly what it is, but intellectually there is no other sociologist who inspires me more than he ... Tilly's way of integrating data across multiple disciplines, the ability to integrate and synthesize information and ideas, to make connections that transcend disciplinary and academic boundaries." The parallels between Ms. Ali and Tilly provide interesting insights on Ms. Ali and Islam. The world changed for many and certainly for Ms. Ali after 9/11. Instead of moving away from Islam, she became a scholar of Islamic identity and leadership. Ms. Ali began a period of self-exploration to try and understand this act of violence by reading Tilly's work on identity and social boundaries.

Tilly (2006) examines identity in terms of relationships with others and the shifts they undergo over time or as a result of one incident in time. Ms. Ali's experience immediately after 9/11 could be that one incident in time. She shifted her research to understanding the Muslim diaspora against the backdrop of negativity. Intellectually and personally, Ms. Ali questioned identity and spirituality within the Muslim community. Tilly's book *Why?* (2006) explores reasons for the attack through the eyes of journalists on the ground and the street-level tenacity of survivors at the World Trade Center. This conversation and the connections to Tilly gave me new insights into Ms. Ali's view of the world. She observes the world from an intellectual perspective and through periods of reflection. Given the geographic distance between us, we did not meet frequently but maintained an open dialogue and correspondence via email or Skype. Although we "talked" frequently, I struggled to understand Ms. Ali's perspective, and felt the distance between us. I kept referring to my notes and reflecting on her story. Originally, I had tossed Tilly aside, but as I thought more on Ms. Ali and the 9/11 stories, I felt the need to read Tilly's book. I have since studied a fair amount of his work, and in the process, I came to know Tilly and slowly began to see what Ms. Ali was about. Reading Tilly's *Why?* led me to think more deeply about her view of the world. Tilly and Ali were both searching for answers and reasons for 9/11 but from two completely different perspectives. In my opinion, this search created a moment of realization and a shift in her life and her views of Islam.

Ms. Ali and Tilly ask the same question from different angles to explore the bigger question of "Why?" Tilly explores these reasons through Muslim identity, looking through the prism of US media and FBI profiling, whereas Ms. Ali searches for understanding by researching Muslim communities living outside their home country. Both weave together disparate disciplines to understand complex social issues. Amid increasingly negative press, Ms. Ali searches for the positive side of Muslim leadership. The widespread hostility of Muslims continues today, with fears about the rise of secular Arab nationalists and the power of the Muslim Brotherhood. Such angst is representative of "our own mental hobgoblins" left over from memories of 9/11 (Kristoff 2011, 9). Tilly adds to the confusion around Muslim leadership, commenting on al-Qaeda, Islam, and the global reach of terrorism. He depicts terrorist leaders as motivated by "a combination of spiritual, emotional, and material rewards which meet the needs of people who are already seeking to participate in simplifying and purifying the world" (Tilly 2006, 169). These words are often linked with transformational leadership (Ciulla 2004; Eagly 2007). The word "purification," is rarely linked to transformational leaders, but in discussions of leadership, someone is bound to ask whether Hitler, Saddam Hussein, or Pol Pot were transformational leaders (Ciulla 2004). Given such questions, scholars define transformational leadership as highlighting ethics of character, authenticity, and often spirituality while aiming for the greater good (Ciulla 2004; Knapp 2007; Dent et al. 2005).

Searching for Purpose

Turning to sociology, Ms. Ali discovered herself, uncovering multiple layers of culture, religion, and spirituality. Driven by personal questions and historical events, she found in this intellectual pursuit a path of discovery. Her research provided insight and helped further define her relationship with Islam. At university she was often asked to explain Islam and the third world. "It gave me an opportunity to learn more about the religion I had inherited in a more intellectual way, and this was important for me because it allowed me to appreciate Islam and the Muslim community in ways I had never thought about." In particular, 9/11 was the fillip for understanding "exactly who I was and what I wanted to do." She turned down medical school to pursue a PhD in sociology. Although being a doctor would have filled the need to serve others and provide financial support for her family, something inside gnawed at her, and she started to question medical school, wrestling with her conscience and her inner picture of herself as "the daughter who always obeyed and never got angry." At this point she made a decision to pursue sociology "to explore the other side of me." Ms. Ali was very much aware that this decision would result in an emotional struggle within her family.

Bangladeshi culture is hierarchical, emphasizing deference and avoidance of confrontations, particularly with parents (Ehsan 2002). Ms. Ali felt the need to place both a physical and emotional distance between herself and her parents in order to reconcile these disparate parts of self. "To maintain the person I was becoming, I had to move away and maintain this distance. I was slowly bridging the 'me' that I was becoming and the 'me' that they knew." Remaining at school and studying for a PhD was a way to avoid family obligations. By the time she turned 20, her mother called weekly to ask about marriage prospects and dates. "I wasn't certain I wanted to be married or have children." In the summer breaks, she travelled to Bangladesh, but by the third year she no longer wanted to make the trip. "I did not want to see my parents, and I started feeling guilty. I was thrilled to get on the plane to leave, but once on the plane I started to feel guilty." She spoke to her parents infrequently. When she did, the conversations were frustrating and filled with "anger that I had never expressed before."

Moments of Realization

This confrontational period eventually led to reconciliation for Ms. Ali—internally and with her parents. "It was really important for me to become comfortable with conflict and learn how to communicate instead of being resentful or submissive." This painful period helped her "accept myself and understand and accept them." Guilt and tension led to growth. She explained, "If I hadn't moved away and changed professional directions, I would not have learned this. The distance helped define myself and take responsibility for that definition. Prior to this, I used to define myself in relation to the 'other,' external forces, and specifically my family. The problem was not only about finding myself; I needed to take responsibility for who I am and what I was doing. I could not blame anybody else now for constraining my choices. I had to choose and accept the consequences. This long period of reflection and rejecting everything I knew was enlightening."

She went through many internal conversations searching for a purpose; yet her drive and "I'll show you" behavior took over, and things started to settle into place. This period was fraught with emotional upheaval, struggling with family expectations, and balancing the need to be true to herself. A regular theme from this reflective period was learning about self, spirituality, and identity. There is a clear sense of "I must know myself before I can express myself" from this story, and many moments altered the course of who she was to become. Three moments in particular stand out: experiencing violence in Toronto, postponing medical school, and returning to Bangladesh. When I asked her about these moments of realization, she added one more: marriage.

Women generally spend more time than men exploring spirituality as a dimension of leadership (Coughlin et al. 2005; Buck 2007; Ibarra 2005). As midlife approaches, some women struggle to meet expectations from the external world while also grappling with questions of meaning. Their questions are internally focused—to find purpose and uncover who they truly want to be. This quest and subsequent questions are vital steps in leadership. High levels of self-awareness are critical cornerstones of leadership, and the midlife period for women provides the platform for this development (Ciulla 2004; Coughlin et al. 2005). Ms. Ali's journey of self-discovery began earlier than midlife, which may be due to cultural pressures, along with the impact of 9/11and its aftermath.

Despite leading a peripatetic life, Ms. Ali's traditional values remained part of the family fabric. She was never required to wear a veil, but in her family there was a *mental* purdah; that is, roles were assigned based on tradition. For many Bangladeshi families, wearing a purdah goes beyond sartorial requirements and into belief systems. Purdah philosophy permeates social roles, female seclusion, and arranged marriages (Sultana et al. 2009). Ms. Ali took off her "dutiful daughter veil" and moved away from parental expectations and cultural traditions toward an intellectual pursuit of self-discovery. The decision to postpone medical school was a relief, the first painful step after years of conflict with her parents. "Becoming a doctor was not really about me. I had been doing that for others," Ms. Ali remarked. With this change in direction she felt better about herself, but the decision drove a wedge between her and her family.

Ms. Ali believes change is possible through education. Education, knowledge, and reading have become her lifeline and value-drivers. The drive to eradicate poverty and emancipate women through education is one of the reasons Ms. Ali returned to Bangladesh. Remarkably, Bangladesh began substantial economic shifts by enabling women to start businesses with microloans, through education and employment ("Bangladesh Out of the Basket," *Economist* 2012). The contradictions between this and purdah mentality remain entrenched in Bangladesh, often clashing with Sheikh Hasina's educational empowerment for women. In Bangladesh women are raised to obey their fathers and remain dependent on their husbands; they are not allowed to leave the house, own property, or find work. For some, the purdah illustrates family status and Islamic rules, and for others the purdah represents restrictions holding women back. A few see the purdah as a way to follow Islamic rules, protect modesty, provide safety, and indicate wealth while not necessarily hindering advancement (Sultana et al. 2009).

One of Ms. Ali's family's clear expectations—and her obligation—was marriage. She was in her twenties when the topic arose, and stopped answering her mother's phone calls. Marriage was another moment of realization and turning point. Throughout our interviews, Ms. Ali refers to her husband's influence on her life and leadership style. She credits her husband (a French Canadian she met at university) with changing her leadership style in recent years. "His experience and deep understanding of human relations has influenced me tremendously in taking on a leadership style that is participatory and emphasizes facilitation of others' talents and strengths and letting others discover their strengths. Marriage has shifted my perspective on how I want to live my life and what are my priorities in terms of career and even how I take my professional journey." Ms. Ali has come full circle; she struggled with Islam in high school, examined values in college, and in graduate school questioned family and challenged traditions and expectations. A conference in Montreal changed everything. "I went from being a person who never wanted to get married to meeting my husband-to-be for the first time."

Education, Leadership, and Change

In Bangladesh, the role of women in leadership positions is somewhat confusing. The Koran and politics are the two main contributing factors, and Muslim leadership among women is even more complex. This confusion stems from early Islamic philosophy, which offered more rights to women than today's version does. Historical data suggest that early Islam, before the seventh century, offered more rights to women. In the Koran women, in traditional roles, hold an honored and respected position. There were (are) specific laws, customs, and cultural norms that applied to women. Subsequently, evidence suggests that patriarchal social systems and conservative thinking influenced modern Islam's views on women's status. Scholars examining the Koran found citations describing the rights of men and women equally. In addition, they also found that, "even though women have rights similar to those of men, they are inferior in status; men have authority over women because god made the one superior to the other" (Swenson 2009, 146).

Ms. Ali explained, "Female Muslim leadership ranges from conservatism, secularism, liberalism, loyalty to change and reform." She discussed the differences and complex nature of female Muslim leaders seen in the writings and style differences of Ingrid Mattson, an Islamic scholar from the University of Chicago, and Irshad Manji, an author who writes about the new Islam. Manji calls herself a "Muslim Refusenik" (Manji 2003, 2) searching for reform in the Muslim community or within the religion (Safi 2005; Khan 2005). Mattson, a conservative Muslim, embraces her religion to drive change within the community (Mattson 2005; Peshkova 2009). Manji (2003), a liberal activist, agrees the Koran is pardoxical and argues the need to restore respectable beliefs to ensure Muslim women's empowerment. Manji and Mattson appear to be pursuing the same goal, reexamining leadership and gender within the Muslim community, albeit from very different perspectives.

The debate about equal rights for women under Islam has been marked by confusion due to multiple interpretations of the Koran across many cultures. Sharia law, the moral code of Islam, complements or interprets the scripture, but the rulings vary across Muslim countries. Manji and Mattson both examine Muslim women leaders or the need to have women in leadership positions. Mattson focuses on women in religious leadership positions, specifically in American Muslim communities. Manji, on the other hand, calls for complete reform of her religion and questions leadership. In Malaysia, Marina Mahathir, an advocate for Muslim women, argues for equal rights in Malaysia's Sharia courts and asserts that the new Islamic laws relegates Muslim women to second-class status compared to non-Muslim citizens. All three women highlight the multiple interpretations in the Koran of the role and status of women. Strangely enough with this ongoing dialogue about equal Muslim women in leadership positions, Bangladesh, a predominantly Muslim country, is governed by a woman.

These different opinions reflect the vast range and disparate views on female leadership in the Muslim community outside of Bangladesh. In Bangladesh the situation is more perplexing as the country is a patriarchal society run by a woman, female leadership giving the pretense of equality, but it is a matter of dynastic succession where "kinship trumped gender" (Thompson 2003, 545). Sheikh Hasina's rise to power reinforces the confusion and contradictions: she won an election in 1996, was overthrown in 2001, lived through a grenade attack in 2004, and returned to power in 2006 (Ahmed 2004; Bennett 2010). She was born into a political family; her father was Sheik Mujib Rahman, the founding father of Bangladesh. Sheik Hasina was catapulted into a leadership position after her father's death; the following quote illustrates how she views her role in a patriarchal society:

> Prime Minister Sheikh Hasina was so concerned about her image as a female leader in morally conservative Bangladesh that she refused to be addressed as "madam" (which she felt had dubious connotations). She insisted instead on being addressed as "sir." (Thompson 2003, 552)

I sat in the audience with Ms. Ali in late January 2011, listening to Sheikh Hasina's speech at the women's conference on education in Bangladesh. She emphasized the need to educate women to become the economic drivers of change in order to eradicate poverty, and that empowering women is a top priority for Bangladesh, as well as ensuring more girls graduate from school. If Ms. Ali and Sheik Hasina continue their drive for change, discussions of purdah will be about matters of style rather than of education and empowerment.

A Moral Turning Point

Ms. Ali is a young leader who transmits a strong message of authenticity. Based on my conversations with her, I find she believes strongly in authentic, moral leadership, which is a much needed quality for the next generation of leadership in Bangladesh and across the globe. Ms. Ali shared, "Moral leadership is the essence of who I am and what I believe is important for my students, the future leaders of Bangladesh, and other emerging Asian countries." She pursues work with a bigger purpose, connecting, collaborating, and building "the global common good combining social and intellectual dimensions" (Knapp 2007, xiii). Ms. Ali repeatedly discussed the integration of identity, spirituality, and morality into her whole self—personal and professional. Being true to self and serving others is integral to her life and her realized identity. Ms. Ali rebelled against aspects of her culture which could no longer be reconciled with who she was becoming. Yet she maintained consistency in values, discovering the spiritual nature of leadership and firmly believing in the moral side. This moral compass guides Ms. Ali. She sees her role as facilitator, guide, and mentor, helping to develop the next generation of women leaders.

Concluding Thoughts

Conducting this research, I uncovered events and turning points in Ms. Ali's life, and my own life as well. These moments of realization offer an opportunity to change directions. Thinking about our correspondence, I was most struck by Ms. Ali's journey of self-discovery through an intellectual endeavor or through other significant events. I admired her soul-searching, her deep questioning, and ability to look within herself, an unusual quality in someone so young. Midlife is often equated with the middle years, anywhere from ages of 35–45 and is seen as a time of searching for self (Vickers-Willis 2002; Hargrave 2006). But this is not always the case; soul-searching can begin at any stage of life and is often triggered by significant events. Interestingly enough, a global advertising firm, McCann Erickson recently conducted research on women in Asia and found the so-called midlife years starting at a significantly younger age there than elsewhere.

Ms. Ali views the world from multiple angles, using a combination of philosophical, intellectual, spiritual, and emotional perspectives. Her intellectual and inquisitive nature was apparent at our first meeting, and soon her spiritual and emotional sides began to shine through. I now see that Ms. Ali presented many elements attributed to transformational leadership, specifically servant leadership. Servant leadership and transformational leadership are both linked by ethics and are morally grounded (Ciulla 2004). The servant leader, like the transformational leader, has a positive impact on followers by bringing them to a higher level of performance, understanding, and values. Such leaders are sometimes asked, "What is the[ir] effect on the least privileged in society?" (Ciulla 2004, 17). Looking at Ms. Ali's role and her decision to return to Bangladesh, the answer is obvious. She had many other opportunities, but her school's philosophy and the desire to help others brought her back to Bangladesh. Her goal was to use her leadership skills to facilitate (her choice of words) young Asian women who may not have had the opportunity or financial means to attend school. She appears selfless in her pursuit and tireless in her desire to build the next generation of women leaders, firmly believing this generation can make a difference. Teaching provides her with an opportunity to impact many lives, and she embraces this responsibility unconditionally. She has the ability to affect and shape the thinking of thousands of young women, guiding these emerging leaders with a solid foundation of moral leadership.

Ms. Ali rejected traditions and struggled with identity on many different levels, but today she is "home" in Bangladesh, in a country which she never thought she would return. I asked her "What should leadership look like for your students and for the future of Bangladesh?" She responded: "It will depend on how well we teach our students and what choices they make. In the end, it will have to be their choice, but I hope it looks like what you call transformational leadership—leading with compassion, empathy, integrity, and participation. I hope my students will be able to lead in a way that makes them prioritize service to those they are leading or representing, rather than putting their own personal interests first. Will it look like that? I do not know."

"The Chinese person is a totality of social roles; without a network one is no one. The individual is organized and motivated by the 'other' (if not the 'nation' then the 'family'), regarding himself as the instrument of the others." (Sun Longji 1989, 31)

In Chinese culture from birth on, each person is enclosed by a network of interpersonal relationships that define and organize existence. One's circle or sodality is essential for mutual assistance, as well as for the definition of self. (Pellow 1993, 32–33)

CHAPTER 4

Judy Lee's Story: Out of Asia and into Africa

You can't cross a river without getting wet.

Zulu Proverb

Judy Lee is an impeccably dressed Taiwanese businesswoman in her late thirties. I interviewed Ms. Lee in December 2010 in Hong Kong and continued our meetings and correspondence until mid-2012. I was introduced to Ms. Lee through a former business colleague in Hong Kong. Ms. Lee and I always met in the Four Seasons Hotel lobby or in an upscale European coffee house in Hong Kong's central business district. Ms. Lee is the poster child for understated luxury, a legacy left over from her work with luxury brands. Sitting in the Four Seasons surrounded by the power brokers of Hong Kong's banking community, Ms. Lee is thousands of miles away from the dirt roads of Nigeria where she previously worked for a global consumer products company. The waiters address her in Cantonese, but she immediately responds in English. Today she is a freelance consultant for a variety of US consumer brands, helping them with market entry strategies and business transformation.

Born in Taiwan, Ms. Lee has worked in high-powered strategic marketing roles for national and multinational corporations in South Africa, Nigeria, Kenya, Hong Kong, and China; she is fluent in English, Chinese, and Japanese. The values of education and ongoing learning, conforming to society, respecting integrity and family were instilled in her by teacher parents—a father who taught history and aspired to complete a PhD and a mother who taught home economics and exposed her daughter to the secrets of Taiwanese, Chinese, and Japanese cuisine. While living in South Africa she learned Thai, Italian, and French cooking. Ms. Lee loves to cook, and one of the things she does for colleagues and people on her team, in her church, her friends, and her family is to cook.

Banished to the Republic

She recalled, "Dad left China as a younger man and followed Chiang Kai Shek" (the Chinese opposition leader who fought against Mao Zedong and moved to the island of Taiwan, then called Formosa). "My Dad's family was from Hunan Province, and they were quite well off back there. My father was always proud of the history of China and our region." Life in Taiwan was not easy. Her father never regained the status or material wealth he had on the mainland. He left China with nothing. Ms. Lee says this influenced her determination to get ahead and make her parents proud of her.

In Taiwan Ms. Lee joined a program for young leaders during university summer and winter programs. Her job was to receive delegates and foreign guests and put on seminars to help the Taiwanese government build diplomatic relations. One such delegation came from South Africa, which had maintained diplomatic relations with Taiwan since 1949, the year Mao Zedong rose to power in the People's Republic of China and Chiang Kai Shek was forced retreat to Taiwan (Spence 1990; Fairbank 1992). Ms. Lee benefitted from the diplomatic and economic relationships between Taiwan and South Africa. Since the late 1960s Taiwan has provided economic support to many independent African nations and extended trade and economic ties with South Africa (Pickles and Woods 1989). This expansion included educational exchange programs that have brought delegations and conferences to Taiwan. One of the delegations invited Ms. Lee to attend a youth leadership conference in Johannesburg and Cape Town, along with other delegates from 27 nations, and she remained in the country for two months. Her stay there was coincidentally at the time when Nelson Mandela was being released from prison and preparing for political office.

"I remember speaking to university students and media. My picture was in the paper, and there was much discussion about Mandela. He represented freedom, a voice. I was totally intrigued by him. He not only represented freedom and a voice for his people, but also qualities of resilience and hope for the future." She ended up talking to the University of the Witwatersrand in Johannesburg (or Wits, as it is known locally) about its MBA program, and four years later she moved to South Africa to take the course. "I was intrigued by the MBA professor and unlike the other Chinese attending the leadership conference, I was asking questions. I'm not shy. I started to think about moving to South Africa and when the dean at Wits invited me to study at the university, I thought long and hard about it. While three different United States universities, in New York, Michigan, and California, had accepted me, I eventually decided to go to South Africa instead. They wanted at least five percent international students, and the fees were cheaper! So I joined students from Russia and Turkey. For the first few months I struggled, because all the courses were in English, and I was finding it difficult to keep up as I learned the language at the same time. Whenever my parents called, I cried on the phone."

Ms. Lee's character is a blend of ambivalence and confidence. "Since I was little, I knew I was different, because I liked speaking in front of people and had a stronger sense of justice. But I was not confident, so I used to practice all the time—particularly speaking English, because we only spoke Chinese at home. To give myself an incentive to learn, I took part in an English-speaking contest. The first time I failed, but I didn't give up and tried again the year after. Then I was selected as one of the winners qualifying for a two-month English intensive training program by the Taiwanese education ministry."

Driven and Gifted

The experience gave her encouragement. "I discovered I had a passion and a gift, which was very useful when I started working, I can be fearless and courageous though I need to balance these qualities with wisdom. Receiving feedback helps!" On graduation from the MBA program, Ms. Lee had to work out if she wanted to stay or return to Taiwan. While her home was in Taiwan, her heart was now in South Africa, where the world seemed bigger and more opportunities beckoned. She purchased a piece of land and built a home in Johannesburg.

She joined a multinational organization, which initially wanted a Chinese-speaking marketing person in its strategy division to help develop a plan for entering the Chinese market. While she admitted that "I was nervous because I was junior level but giving advice to someone very senior," her confident style and obvious ability soon saw her on a fast track for high-potential executive position. She was given more opportunities and challenges. One project required frequent travel to Kenya to develop a growth plan. She thrived and was rewarded with other increasingly difficult assignments that helped develop her leadership skills. "The fourth month after I joined, I walked into the office of the chief executive officer and handed him a one-pager on myself and what I wanted to do," Ms. Lee said. "It included an outline of where I wanted to go and what I liked to do best. I asked for his help." She is not certain if it was this document or her forthright manner, but soon after that day she was invited to be on a few strategic projects for business exposure and acceleration of learning. "My boss taught me to think about solutions and said he wanted me to help build the company with him. This helped build my leadership skills. He always asked, 'Lee, what do you think?'" She giggled, "For some reason, he always called me Lee never by my first name."

In Kenya, the company wanted new ideas about a market that was saturated with too many products. Ms. Lee produced a high-level analysis and provided the executives with a simple product and pricing framework for growing the market. The company dithered on what direction to take and later engaged a global strategic consulting firm to also ask for global best practice. When it came time to review the plans, hers were almost identical to those of the consultancy. "The fact was," Ms. Lee said, "we had too many brands in the market, and we weren't seeing the returns. The brands were fighting against each other and confusing the customer. And while no one wanted to admit it, we had a credibility issue with the leadership in place." Ms. Lee worked side-by-side with ethnographers from a global strategy firm to find out where and what consumers were buying, what they wanted, and how they viewed her firm's various product offerings. While her colleagues and their competitors were trying to find 2 or 3 percent growth, Ms. Lee sized up the challenge with a bigger question, "How large is the opportunity?" Working around the clock with the consulting firm, Ms. Lee discovered that "trust" was the real issue for staff, management, suppliers, the retail channel, and consumers. Profits were falling because of a lack of trust, and trust was being eroded because profits were falling. Ms. Lee realized this was a never-ending circle of tribal and cross-cultural challenges between the team and the distributors. She built a model around trust and how customers related to products, and refocused everyone on the consumer experience. "It was a tremendous training ground," she said. Years later, working with a global management consulting firm, she went into Angola and Nigeria, driving cross-country where there were no roads, in pursuit of information about how to organize distribution of products in developing countries.

Culture Shock in the Motherland

The work in Africa was nothing compared with the challenges in China. While her heritage is Chinese, her heart remains in South Africa. Working in China's markets, she had to adapt to the environment quickly and was required to deliver results, and she wanted to make the best use of the opportunity. Ms. Lee shared, "Arriving in Hong Kong, my base for the China market, I experienced significant culture shock. I could not believe how people lived. In Johannesburg, I had a large house, plenty of room, and a garden. In Hong Kong, I was lucky to have a 750-square-feet flat not facing a brick wall. Although I am Chinese, I could not figure out people's behavior. I never questioned my decision to move to China, I was too focused on doing something great. The Olympics were coming up, and I knew our company could make an impact on the market. After arriving in China, travelling across cities I experienced significant cultural shock with the manners of the Chinese at the airport, in the traffic, at the restaurant. However, I never questioned my decision to move to China as there was so much I learned."

While working in China, she thought she had the support of the managing director and a solid network at corporate headquarters in the United States. She faced three challenges: she was young, female, and not as fluent in Chinese as she would have liked. Her [mostly Chinese] employees saw only her "differences" and ridiculed her Chinese. Foreigners (*wai-guo ren*) can be excused for poor language skills, but anyone with a Chinese face and name is rarely forgiven for not knowing the language fluently. Her embarrassment was made worse by her position as second-in-command to the managing director.

Ms. Lee joked about the shock of her transition. "Sometimes when I ran workshops, I had funny Chinese coming out. I spoke so slowly they would laugh at me, but I'd ask them to help me. I would say, 'I'm here to help you, so you can help me also.'" Always up for a challenge, Ms. Lee used anything to get her message across. Language was one issue, but the real challenge was status or lack of it. She shared, "My most challenging meeting was in Sichuan Province, where one old-school Chinese manager ran the business in a military style." Watching this senior leader speak to the employees, she noticed that he did not listen or ignored comments from the staff. She explained, "He was blocking the voices of the direct reports. I could see their reactions through their body language." The purpose of the meeting was to drive change, and the organization needed everyone's opinion and all voices heard. Ms. Lee said, "When they stayed silent, I called the meeting to a halt. I challenged the older Chinese men, asking them why there was no communication happening, no eye contact, and this style of leadership did not embrace our values."

While some may consider this decision inconsequential, this bold move illustrates a cultural difference in leadership styles. Based on my experience working in China, Ms. Lee's decision to stop a meeting with her colleague is not an easy feat, impacting face, hierarchy, and protocol. China may hold the record for more women millionaires and for women in leadership positions, but the country still follows a traditional Confucian hierarchy (Cheung and Halpern 2010; Spence 1990; Fairbank 1992; Chhokar et al. 2008). Respect for hierarchy and the pressure to maintain face are not to be taken lightly (Wang et al. 2005). Ms. Lee's public dressing-down of a colleague could be attributed to spending her formative years working for a US multinational corporation in South Africa. Working for an American firm, Ms. Lee learned leadership from an egalitarian style in which "extreme individualism combined with participative managerial" perspective (Adler 1997, 174).

I asked Ms. Lee about this intervention and whether she recognized the cultural differences in leadership. She responded, "I had no choice but to carry on or lose all impetus for change." As she told the story, I could see she was reliving the experience. Her comments focused on business implications rather than on considering cultural reflections or the softer side of leadership. She continued with, "We walked through the guiding principles about how meetings should work and how no one was embracing the principles. I said we either continue or stop, but if we stop, your area will be known as unco-operative. The body language changed and the mood adjusted. The general manager eventually became a huge supporter. We talked privately later, and the turnaround started from then." Reflecting on this story and other interviews, Ms. Lee vividly recalls business dynamics but did not see how these challenges shaped her leadership and thinking style. Sometimes, I view Ms. Lee as idealistic, a leader firmly believing in management processes particularly when she uses the term "guiding principles" rather than "personal reflection." At other times, she refers to spirituality or religiosity as a source of introspection and calmness. She carries both a practical and spiritual side of leadership but the two sides remains separated. When I discussed the final version of her story with Ms. Lee, she explained, "I am not sure I agree with this. Actually, I engaged in multilevel discussions and requested the parties concerned for reflections, collaborations of where we were and how we were doing…I would note down the dynamics and energy of the groups and senior managers to check in and reflect on the progress of our organization. And what potential intervention program and support could be helpful." While she strives to balance results and empathy, it appears she may lean too heavily on the practical side of performance.

Moments of Realization

There were many moments of realization for Ms. Lee. The first began in college when she understood she needed to learn English to get ahead. "I would walk to school carrying a small tape recorder and listening to Shakespeare." She desperately wanted to improve her English in a Chinese-speaking household. In college she also learned Japanese. She is fluent in Japanese but sees English as providing more opportunities. She enjoyed the arts, culture, and travel; more important. She liked being on stage, that is, center stage. The stage experience provided public speaking confidence and the drive to perfect her English skills. At university she took part in overseas seminars and had her eyes opened to the wider world. Her decision to study business in Johannesburg pushed her boundaries and helped make her flexible, adaptable, and creative. When I asked about her decision to move to South Africa, she said, "Quite frankly... it changed the course of my life."

Hearing this statement, I was not entirely convinced that Ms. Lee realized the incredible journey she had made. Beginning her career after apartheid in South Africa is certainly unconventional. Listening to her experiences, it is hard to picture Ms. Lee (in her current sartorial splendor), donning gum boots and khakis, sitting in the back of a jeep, on the muddy back roads, with a wayward anthropologist and a bookish strategist moving into the unknown territories of Kenya, Angola, and Nigeria. Ms. Lee makes light of these stories and is more excited to discuss the distribution channels rather than cross-cultural adventures. While she recounts the consumers' experiences eating ice cream, my mind conjures up Indiana Jones. I wonder why she is not more excited about these experiences. While she indicates this work experience was a turning point in her life, she remains focused on business outcomes rather than this incredible experience. Our discussion reverts back to my hunch that she struggles with the balance between business results and the softer side of leadership. As Ms. Lee discusses where or how to position products on the storeroom shelf, I find myself struck by the wonderful sense of adventure and the learning achieved in her endeavors. Listening to Ms. Lee, I am intrigued by the adventure and want to hear more about the wilds of Africa, but Ms. Lee is more content or comfortable speaking in terms of business. Upon reflection, is this due to my desire to control the interview, attached to my own thoughts, or to allowing fixed beliefs or bias to enter the situation?

Finding Her Religion

In addition to business, there is another side to Ms. Lee; her face lights up when she talks about religion. Finding God was definitely a moment of realization for her. During a particularly dark period in her life, someone on her team at work asked her to join a prayer meeting. Ms. Lee did not think anything of it and was about to refuse but went along to the meeting anyway. She had recently broken up with her long-term boyfriend and was particularly distraught. "I had been meditating every day, trying to find peace, and reflecting on life," she recalls. "One of my team members used to pray, and I asked her how she did it. She simply took my hand and started to pray. Suddenly I felt the power of prayer." She started to think deeply about love and concluded, "God loves me, and that love will not fail."

From this point on, she became a born-again Christian, redefining herself and finding peace. Ms. Lee believes there is "wisdom in spirituality, which has become a tremendous source of strength. My faith increased especially in the difficult situations. God helped me recognize my gifts." Another moment of realization came during a corporate restructuring with a different company. While her business performed well, she had clashes with a difficult boss from Europe when she was tasked with building up the business in China just prior to the Olympics. In South Africa, she had met this leader on many occasions; she had heard he was tough but thought she could learn from him. After accepting the role in China, in addition to the cultural challenges, she had to deal with two changes. First, she was not given the full authority to run the business in China. Second, her boss changed after the success of the Olympic campaign. Because of not receiving the "full title," she had to balance authority and an assertive style with the hierarchy in China. She mentioned this during meetings with her staff and peers; her boss challenged decisions, questioned her reasoning, and undermined her authority. The entire office felt the tension between the two. Despite—or because of—this she delivered results even with the constant barrage from a difficult boss. This leadership experience took its toll on her, and she decided to leave. When I first met, Ms. Lee she was still reeling from her decision to sign a separation agreement from a company she admired and where she had had an otherwise stellar career.

Reflecting on where she is now and when I first met her, I would call this a moment of realization. She shared many stories with me about her boss, the situation at work, and the emotional impact on her. She remained confident in her abilities but emotionally drained by the experience. This experience highlighted Ms. Lee's analytical thinking. Using her business mind, she shared her decision-making process with me as she embarked on a practical problem-solving methodology to analyze events leading up to her decision to leave the firm. During this decision-making stage, she turned to religion. She spent much time reflecting, reading, and studying the Bible. We spent a lot of time talking about religion or her work, and this focus prompted me to ask if she wanted to study theology and become a spiritual leader. She adamantly replied, "My strengths are in business." As we discussed her current professional challenges and how she coped through these events, she reflected on her time in South Africa. During her lunch break, she took time to "listen to a pastor speak about women and worth, a sense of worth which comes from God. I found quietness and a peace that I had not experienced for a long time. I look at people differently, and they look at me differently." Reflecting on my interviews with Ms. Lee, I can see that religion provides her with the mental space needed to balance a very determined mind, business results, and the human side of leadership. I also feel that Ms. Lee's embrace of religion is similar to the way she used problem solving to analyze her work challenges. In my opinion, religion provided an outlet and effective coping mechanism.

Ms. Lee told me, "As a leader, I know that there are things in my control and things not in my control; it's less stressful now that I don't have to control everything, and I know my 'calling' is in the marketplace. I am in God, and he is in me. He is the center and the anchor of my life." She says this sense of peace helped her with a decision to leave her employer after 12 years. She used the same technique with the breakup of her long-term partner and looked to God for guidance. This break from work gives her time to study leadership, mergers, and acquisitions and to travel to "her dream places." She is active in her church providing coaching to young Christians and taking this time to rethink who she is and where she wants to be.

A Spiritual Turning Point

In Ms. Lee's story, religion, family, community, and fierce determination stand out. Oddly enough, inside organizations, spirituality and religion are not always discussed openly (Lips-Wiersma and Mills 2002). There are strong ties between spirituality and leadership, as both are joined together through a journey of self-discovery. There are also clear links between women, spirituality, and leadership (Nadoff 2005; Wingard 2005; Buck 2007; Bateson 2000). Religion provides Ms. Lee with a bridge to balance the external working world and internal pressures of driving success. This belief system provided support during her years in South Africa, China, and Hong Kong as she was working through the challenges that have surfaced and dealing with those that remained submerged (Lips-Wiersma and Mills 2002; Korac-Kakabadse et al. 2002). During our interviews, Ms. Lee frequently brought up her religious beliefs and described leadership as similar to answering "a call." She refers to work as "her calling in the markets." A calling can simply mean having awareness, yet it is more frequently used with organized religions to represent a purposeful life with meaning, direction, and membership (Komives 2005).

Listening to Ms. Lee and thinking about her story, I noticed that she fluctuates between holding onto business performance and sitting back and allowing change to unfold rather than intervening and controlling. She admits that earlier in her career, she was more directive and controlling, but whether through development or spiritual reflection, she has moved toward a coaching style of leadership. Her leadership style is now more focused on coaching and helping others. One of her passions is cooking, and she often cooks lavish meals for her team. She believes in connecting with her team and bringing them into her personal life. While not explicitly stated, she alluded to building a connection between her church community, her team, and her family. She embraces religion completely, giving the impression of an evangelist, but she is aware that she has to hold back rather than try to convert everyone.

Ms. Lee's career started in what is traditionally known as a male-dominated work environment. Her childhood drive to find her voice, to be heard and be on stage, provided a solid ground for success in this environment. This fierce determination to succeed is her driver. This success focus will stand her in good stead for a career with another multinational organization. Her work experience and stretching assignments in South Africa provided the early leadership training necessary to build diverse teams, and her personal drive delivers business results. Ms. Lee has no problem asking for help; she knows what she wants to achieve and has always found a mentor and coach to help her advance quickly through the corporate ranks.

She also credits family as her "source of comfort, love, and support. My mother is concerned that I am not working and still living in Shanghai." She is very close to her parents and her 94-year-old grandmother, and Ms. Lee regularly travels back and forth from Shanghai to Taiwan to spend time with her family and seeks advice and consults her parents before making any career decisions. Having lived away from Taiwan for many years, she nevertheless continues to turn to her family for a solid foundation of support. In Confucian culture, family extends beyond mother and father, and history shows previous generations hold more power than government, organization, or church. Family represents all living and deceased relatives providing guidance and emotional support along with rules of conduct (Winfield et al. 2000)

In my opinion, Ms. Lee's varied experiences and coming out the other side of a difficult work situation unscathed have burnished her leadership potential. She was on the right track until sidelined by a challenging boss and a changing organization. This will not hold her back. Her experiences, coupled with her commitment to make a difference and her determination to succeed will put her in excellent position for the next opportunity. After being away from her home country for over a decade, she has relocated to Taiwan since our interviews began. She continues to provide strategic advice to multinational organizations entering Asia and has also started working with her family's firm on marketing and brand strategies.

For Ms. Lee, making a difference is not about saving the world but about building a humane work environment and, she would add, one with stellar profits and performance. She believes God has a plan for her life, and her vision now is to positively impact over one million global leaders through her consulting work, combining workplace, community, and family. Ms. Lee's leadership style is not only shaped by her company and her religious beliefs, but also by thousands of years of Chinese culture. Reflecting on her own style, Ms. Lee says she has changed, and her personal circumstances have changed, but she sees herself as a visionary able to bring change through both listening and leading. She is firmly placed in the center with two guiding forces for support: family and religion. As she moves forward with her new vision, the circle includes employees and community, and all are linked to work and interests. Her advice to others is: "Don't let negative people stand in your way or kill your passion or your dreams."

Concluding Thoughts

As I reflect on this story and our many meetings, rather than project thoughts on leadership I feel the need to meet Ms. Lee again in a couple of years to see where she lands. Her resilience, her ability to reflect on the experience and journey forward will provide insights into her leadership style. In my opinion she has the intelligence, drive, and determination to succeed. Through the course of our interviews, I am unable to pull out elements of transformational leadership. She has the capability to lead, but her style and analytical thinking may be more suited to directing others rather than to participating and collaborating. That being said, I am aware that she coaches many young women leaders. This coaching focuses on balancing life and career coaching within her religious community. Instead of focusing on aspects of transformational leadership, Ms. Lee's story presented insights into the *how* of leadership through determination, strategic thinking, and staying connected with family and religion. In reviewing the draft of this story, Ms. Lee added one final remark, "My parents and sisters are always encouraging me to live my dreams. They have always been there to support me during my bad times. They are open-minded, comforting, reaffirming who I am, and assure me that things can only get better."

CHAPTER 5

Sara Chin's Story: The Accidental Leader

> At work, you think of the children you've left at home. At home, you think of the work you've left unfinished. Such a struggle is unleashed within yourself, your heart is rent.
>
> *Golda Meir*

Ms. Sara Chin is a tall Singaporean business leader in her midforties with a strong voice and humble spirit. She studied chemical engineering and began her career in consumer products, at the right time at the right place, and she never looked back. Her career and the list of her life achievements are humbling. She moved steadily to leadership roles, and at the outset was offered new opportunities every other year. She attributes her success to hard work and making a choice to become a leader. Ms. Chin started her career in sales and worked her way up the corporate ladder, remaining with the same company for over 18 years. Ms. Chin has achieved many firsts: the first managing director of a global firm, the first woman on a corporate board, and other milestones, but she doesn't place much emphasis on them. She leads a multimillion dollar function, sits on prominent boards, participates in community events, and is an active mother and accomplished athlete. Ms. Chin is a leader with quick eyes and a hearty laugh.

When I was consulting for a global conglomerate, I was introduced to Ms. Chin through the former head of the human resource department. The firm had many lines of business; I was consultant to one of the divisions and at times had interacted with Ms. Chin. I did not work directly with Ms. Chin but worked with many of her colleagues. We were both active in women business networks and connected with an NGO board focusing on women, education, and welfare. In late 2009, Ms. Chin was the keynote speaker for a conference on women in business where I was one of the facilitators. I had heard about Ms. Chin through business contacts and within the community and was delighted that she had time and interest to participate in this research. I interviewed Ms. Chin in early 2010, and we continued our dialogue throughout that year. In 2011, the company went through a significant restructuring resulting in a leadership change and executives leaving the firm. During this upheaval, I lost contact with Ms. Chin, and we have only reconnected in 2012. Given her travel schedule, we met three times for face-to-face interviews, and the remainder of the time corresponded through email, text messages, and phone calls.

Uneasy Beginnings

I met Ms. Chin in 2010 on a steamy Singapore afternoon. Sitting in the brightly lit conference room, chilled by the subzero air-conditioning, I sipped Chinese tea and waited for her arrival. She was running a few minutes late, but as she entered the room, she extended her hand to give me a firm shake. Moving toward the table, she placed her iPhone face down next to her notebook to avoid the constant message pings. Her presence filled the room, and there was no doubt she was in charge. Impeccably dressed, with perfectly manicured hands, she wore a black diamond ring and matching earrings. She had a strong voice and affable manner.

As her iPhone constantly buzzed, she apologized and put the device on silent/vibrate mode. Pointing to her phone, she giggled, "I am addicted. But this device keeps me balanced."

Her schedule would fatigue anyone, but she believes any and all sports activities provide a counterbalance to work and give the necessary energy to be successful. It is hard to fathom how she manages everything. "Early in life I was forced to rely on the support of family and friends. This realization has stayed with me, and I know you cannot get through life without others." Ms. Chin's father died suddenly when she was five years old, moving her from daughter to leader in the family overnight, reinforcing the values of hard work, education, and competition. She grew up rapidly and learned the meaning of the Buddhist and Confucian values that became the foundation for her life. The biggest influences in her life were her mother and sports.

"With sports, you find out a lot about your relationships with people. You can't win without teamwork. You learn to work together as a team. You learn competitiveness, discipline, and never giving up. Frankly, I don't remember what I studied at school—but I certainly remember the medals I won. You learn values in sports that you cannot get from academe. I came from a single-parent family—the biggest influence in my life was my mom." Widowed at the age of 30, her mother never remarried. "A single woman with four children, the second youngest was one...at that time I didn't realize how young it was until I reached my thirties." Her mother instilled a sense of responsibility and hard work in her. Ms. Chin stated, "She has raised us well, to make sure that I knew I had to study hard, I always did well in school—to take care of her—so actually of the siblings, out of the four of us, three went to university. Quite amazing for a single mom, and all of us turned out quite successful in our own way."

Working her way through college, Ms. Chin learned the art of resilience and the perseverance to excel. "If you ask the single biggest influence in terms of values in my life, it is my mom, so she's still strong and healthy, and we make sure we bring her for holidays." Deep in thought, I realize this was the most private side to Ms. Chin, and she added, "That's my very personal side, I don't mind sharing it. I think because I didn't grow up with a silver spoon. In some ways I guess I'm hard working, since young." Out of her personal tragedy the learning she created a leadership style centering on inclusion, helping others, and above all, hard work.

Balancing Life and Work

Curious about how she juggles work and four children, I asked, "How do you find the balance?" Ms. Chin chuckled. "I don't sleep. . . .Just kidding." She believes "integration" is the key in balancing family, work, and community. "I am a mother of four, and I make certain my kids are equally active—when I train, they train. I encourage my team to get involved too." The late Israeli Prime Minister Golda Meir once said "women worry about children when they are at work and worry about work when they are at home." This is not the case with Ms. Chin and elsewhere in Asia where the family is able to step in and help. Ms. Chin's sister, in-laws, and her mother all live with her, and she has two domestic helpers, "amahs" or "aunties." One has been with her for ten years, and both are treated like members of the family. This inclusive integrated balance extends beyond the workday. Her team has become part of Ms. Chin's sporting life, community work, and family events.

Her modesty as a leader springs from an understanding of her place in this world: "I see myself as a business person, a mother, a wife, and a daughter." Her weekends are sacred. "Early in my career, I had a boss who expected a response within 24 hours and for me to be on call every weekend. I didn't enjoy that treatment and will never do that." She juggles family commitments, attends her daughter's theater performance at school in the afternoon, or negotiates a multimillion dollar project; at ease in all these situations, she has both feet firmly planted on the ground.

While Ms. Chin projects a business image during the interviews, her identity is not tied to her role. There are many facets to her life. This is true of many women leaders. Ms. Chin identifies her job as just one aspect of who she is (Helgesen 1995). Ms. Chin achieves great loyalty through giving autonomy and building trust and through her genuine and authentic style. "Unless you get the trust and respect of the people you lead, they won't do what you ask—and why should they? I learned early on in my career the value of hiring talented people and giving them room to grow." Working for a micromanaging boss early in her career taught her to be more open, inclusive, and empathetic with others. "As a result, I don't micromanage or breathe down people's necks. Some people think women are more meticulous and more micromanagers, but I certainly think this is just a stereotype that is not accurate."

Participative and Collaborative

She believes in sharing power, in encouraging participation, and in listening. She achieves her vision by taking her team along with her, rather than by being autocratic. Her cultural upbringing, early life events, and experiences with bosses having different managerial styles helped shape her inclusive, participative, and collaborative leadership style. "I have also been fortunate to work for leaders who trust me. This is the key to good leadership." She believes in providing enough distance and guidance in order to allow her team to perform and move ahead. "Our company is very focused on management by objectives. We are still a manufacturing center for the world. We all have targets, and particularly now, in tougher economic times, if you miss your target, you're gone. The reality now is about making our numbers." Thanks to spending over 18 years with the same firm, she learned and believes leadership is always about performance. "No performance, no job." She does not believe gender is a barrier and does not think it is unusual for a woman to be running a large business: "I do not subscribe to the concept of 'glass ceiling.' Either you make it or you don't. There are only so many places at the top."

Ms. Chin shrugs off her success as accidental and lucky, but it is clear that she has been diligent and has developed the habit of life-long learning. Ms. Chin is known in her industry, her community, in Singapore, and in Asia. Starting in sales, she moved to a country leadership role, then regional, working across product lines and divisions. The business grew significantly, and in many ways these early wins and opportunities provided essential leadership development for her. She feels fortunate to be part of a company that has valued career development. Although development programs in her organization are rare today, Ms. Chin was the recipient of many such programs, including an MBA from a prestigious university funded by the company. Last year, she embarked on an executive coaching program. She is a generous leader who gives her time to others. She feels comfortable coaching and mentoring young leaders inside and outside her organization: "I think it's the nurturing mother in me." After retiring from corporate life, she plans to be a coach. She takes the time both inside and outside her organization to mentor and coach rising stars. "Perhaps it is my maternal side, but after 20-plus years of managing people I find I can bring my own experience to younger managers. Maybe this could be a second career for me?"

In addition to her family experience, Ms. Chin is also different from her Asian counterparts in that her experience has been within the same American multinational company for close to two decades. She views every event as a learning opportunity and is willing to take a risk to prove she can meet any challenge. When I asked about her view on cultural and gender approaches to business, she provided clear-cut examples. She remembered that during promotion announcements the women who received them would ask, "Why me?" and her male colleagues would ask, "Why not me?" In the teams she managed, she noticed that men were more assertive about what they wanted. Ms. Chin wonders why women do not ask for what they want or deserve. She understands from personal experience the challenges with family and career: "Like it or not, especially in Asia, women are the main caretakers of the family, particularly families with young children." She added, "Women feel they can't balance with their family. They don't think they can cope, sometimes I think they can cope, and I believe they are better at coping than they think. Women are the best multitaskers. Men are a single go [working on one thing at a time] while women are trained in multiple roles at any one time." Clarifying this remark, Ms. Chin explains that she means that some men are more comfortable and successful working on a single task or project, whereas women are able to and maybe more adept at working on multiple tasks at once. Ms. Chin believes Singaporean women are privileged with equal opportunity in education and work.

Women Don't Ask

When Ms. Chin addressed a Women in Business workshop in Singapore in late 2009, her opening lines were bold. She entered the room, looked around, walked straight to the front, and asked, "Why don't any of you ask for a promotion?"

At first, the audience, sitting comfortably sipping lattes surrounded by plates of fresh fruit and freshly baked croissants, giggled.

"I am serious," she said. "Let me tell you what happens every month in my office. The men come into my office, sit down, and say, 'Right. I am ready to be promoted to vice president.' Whether or not they have the credentials, they still ask."

More giggles.

"The women come in and say, 'What is the next project I can work on?'"

She studied the crowd and asked, "Project?"

Louder laughs. A few nervous coughs.

"But not one asks to be promoted. Why? This needs to change— ask for what you want and deserve."

Silence ensued as the women in the diverse group from China, Malaysia, Singapore, India, and France smiled, nodded, looked down, or looked away—all avoiding eye contact.

No one said a word or asked Ms. Chin a question.

Watching this performance as a spectator in the audience, I know the answer to this question—stigma and perhaps culture. I, too, have wondered why women don't ask. Thinking about this question, I have asked myself the same thing and realized the reasons for my hesitancy. I watched a number of women, including myself, fall from grace after asking for a promotion or for an increase in compensation. Research into negotiation skills and women indicates a fear of reprisal, stigma, and bias with women who pushed for a promotion or more money (Bowles et al. 2007). Oddly enough, once rejected, women show a reluctance to return to the bargaining table.

Women are penalized more than men in salary negotiations (Bowles and Babcock 2008). Women are viewed as nice, collaborative, and communal; therefore, asking for more or asserting such a claim does not fit the prevailing perceptions (Eagly 2007). Such a priori assumptions regarding modesty and niceness can lead to a slippery slope for women when negotiation and self-promotion are called for. Women I have worked with and interviewed in the course of this research often comment, "Being Asian, we cannot ask." This is a double-edged sword as the drawbacks to not asking often result in women not moving forward. The stigma and cultural overload across Confucian cultures makes asking all the more challenging for Asian women. Now, oddly enough, Ms. Chin knows this and does not see the "not asking for what you deserve" as particularly Asian. She believes women globally have a noticeable tendency not to ask. Sadly, she is correct (Bowles and Babcock 2008; Eagly 2007). But this leaves me wondering why she asked the question in the first place?

Identity

When I asked about her heritage, Ms. Chin indicated that she is Chinese and then immediately stated she is Singaporean. "Yes, of course, I am Singaporean," and her voice trailed off. Looking up from my notebook, I took note of the separation of culture and am reminded of Jayne Ifekwunigwe's book *Scattered Belongings* (1999). Referring to James Baldwin's *Notes of a Native Son*, Ifekwunigwe says, "We cannot escape our origins, however hard we try. Those origins which contain the key—could we but find it—to all that we later become" (Ifekwunigwe 1999, 57). My question about origin and identity elicits a variety of responses from the study participants. Given the history of Singapore, Ms. Chin's response is not unusual. Singapore presents a fascinating mix of heritage, race, and culture; it was a British colony, occupied by the Japanese, and was part of Malaya until independence in 1965. Links with China began in the late 1800s with a million of Chinese escaping rebellion and strife on the mainland by emigrating to Singapore. Given the influx of Chinese, the Qing dynasty established an embassy in Singapore in 1873, ostensibly to watch over the millions of wealthy new emigrants (Spence 1990). Many Singaporean women I have met responded the same way to the question on identity, either claiming links with Malaysia or China despite having lived in Singapore for over 30 years or more. Ms. Chin's Chinese heritage rings through, weaving family into every conversation, making evident the strong social bonds and solid sense of responsibility to parents. In a Chinese family filial piety, respect for family and ancestors, prevail, specifically the eldest son is raised to obey the father, adhering to strict patterns of authority and tradition. Unlike North American culture, Chinese culture gives family priority over the individual, with a reciprocal responsibility of duty. Historically, the family system in China has provided strength while also breeding passivity (Fairbank 1992). Some view filial piety as male dominated, but Ms. Chin's case is different. In the Chin family, women do not have inferior status.

Moments of Realization

Being placed as the leader in the family influenced the person Ms. Chin is today. Ms. Chin believes her success comes from hard work and a desire to learn. But she does not believe in too much planning for the future because "you never know what might happen." Unlike many of her colleagues, she does not hesitate to ask for more responsibility or a promotion. She believes that if there is no challenge, it is time to move on. Once she figures something out or becomes too comfortable, she looks for something different and never seems to run out of energy to learn something new. She learned to dive many years ago, but last year she started diving again and indicated that it is the only place where she truly absorbs the quiet nature of the ocean. As she put it, "I can't bring my iPhone 50 meters deep" (but she might when technology designs a waterproof gadget).

My Moment of Realization

As I reflect on Ms. Chin, I sometimes felt myself on shaky ground in my interpretation of stories and events (Armitage and Gluck 2002). My preconceived notions of leadership and how US multinationals work confused my thinking. When I arrived for our interviews with the full intention of learning more about Ms. Chin, I was often sidelined by the physicality of the interview space. I again think back to my corporate years, buzzwords collide with my thoughts. I am struck by her words "management by objectives," a mental slap hard enough to register on my face. She accurately acknowledges my reaction: "I know this sounds like a cliché." She read my thoughts, as that was exactly what I was thinking. The banal management terms, such as "management by objectives" or "open-door policy," hit a nerve with me, distorting my view. As I listened, my thoughts floated back to boardrooms and tired faces, drooping eyelids, people fiddling with digital devices and whispering to each other: "When is this meeting over?" These fleeting memories of my own corporate experiences flash across my face. As Ms. Chin's values are displayed in our interviews, there were times when I questioned the veracity of her comments based on her use of management speak. In hindsight, this is my own bias. Ms. Chin believes the multinational company in which she has spent her career has shaped her leadership style. The company supported her development through challenging assignments and leadership training. She acknowledges learning from many great bosses as well as from not-so-great people. Her competitive nature in sports has strong links with leadership. Running a large organization successfully requires the ability to build strong teams, and taking part in team sports provides insights in coaching others, navigating power, and overcoming failure (Parker-Pope 2010). In building her team, she deliberately surrounds herself with people who she says are better than she is. She allows them ample opportunity for growth, and her driving force is honesty, particularly in dealing with others. Her leadership philosophy is grounded in sincerity and integrity. Reflecting on my interactions with her, I do not recall any time when Ms. Chin's sincerity, integrity, and honesty did not ring true.

Building a Connected Web of Inclusion

When I asked her what the secret to her success was, she firmly responded, "Family. I involve them in everything I do. I have to give credit to my husband and my family for support." Ms. Chin's life is completely integrated. She does not see work and personal life as either/or—you work or you play. She believes that becoming a parent has significantly added to her awareness of actions and words. At work, her focus on people is visible and another link to the philosophy of inclusion she espouses. She is known for taking time to listen and has built a loyal, engaged team. Every quarter (or three months) Ms. Chin organizes afternoon teas; these are relaxed, comfortable affairs with strong, sweet *kopi* (local coffee) and hot buttered toast with *kaya* (egg and coconut jam). She randomly selects 10 to 12 people, and opens her door for dialogue, without an agenda. In her view, the afternoon teas are an old-fashioned way of "reaching out to the ground."

Ms. Chin insists that she would not be able to run her business or her family without this integrated and inclusive web. This approach is particularly well suited to the collectivist cultures of Asia and global organizations with vast tentacles and multiple links across relationships. Ms. Chin's connected web spins together, like the tightly strung links and chains of her racing bike, a leadership style that reflects life. Family plays an integral role, creating a balanced and humane work environment (Helgesen 1995). This integrated way of leading aligns naturally with Asian values and how organizations in the 21st century work, that is, globally diverse and virtually connected. Reflecting on Ms. Chin, she embraces and embodies this leadership style, not cut off but joined up bringing family and work together. With more women in the workforce, this interconnected way of leading provides a platform of balance. According to Ms. Chin, "it is no longer either or" work and life are inextricably connected.

Concluding Thoughts

Reflecting on Ms. Chin's story, the links to family and authenticity come through first. While she exhibits many qualities of transformational leadership, this story is more about the "how" of leadership. Her story on building an integrated web offers a balanced, calm approach to work and life, one that is based on her integrated web of inclusion, which not only provides the flexibility she needs to balance or integrate life but also benefits her team and family. Research on Asian women lists tradition, culture, and family as persistent hurdles in obtaining and sustaining leadership success (Tuminez 2012; Hewlett and Rashid 2011). Ms. Chin's story illustrates the opposite. She carries a moral obligation to her family, team, and community, which emanates from early life experiences and events. Her strong family values, humble spirit, and competitive drive come through with every meeting.

I did not find a spiritual element in our conversations but did find a strong moral dimension and competitive spirit. This competitive edge began early in life through sports activities at school and has carried over into her work. Ms. Chin sets a high bar for herself and others to exceed. Ms. Chin does not need to ask others for trust; she is easily trusted by a loyal group of followers, not only in these interviews. Her reputation in the community is one of authenticity—what you see is what you get. She is comfortable in her own skin, exudes confidence and composure.

The next chapter brings the participants together in a fictitious setting to engage the reader and experience organizational dynamics, workplace politics, with women at the center stage.

CHAPTER 6

A Corporate Fable

This chapter uses a fictionalized format, bringing the four participants together to discuss organizational dynamics. The fable is real, but the names have been changed to maintain anonymity. The story arose from my earlier Multinational Corporations (MNC) work as head of organizational development, where I facilitated workshops in "organizational savvy," one of the many names for workplace politics. The original intent of this fictionalized format was to gain insights about cross-cultural differences. The result, however, uncovered various reflections of the participants' work experience and organizational culture, rather than of national culture.

The use of narrative fiction is engagingly interactive; the reader can gain deeper insights from multiple perspectives (Speedy 2008; Trahar 2011; Brown and Rhodes 2005). To be clear, my participants did not join together to discuss this corporate fable. Nor do they know one another. Up to this chapter, their stories have remained within each specific chapter. This corporate fable provides a way for researcher, participants, and reader to gain knowledge independently.

The story developed around a fictitious character, Amy, a consumer insights professional. The verbatim comments captured demonstrate multiple perspectives on a common organizational situation. Understandably, using a fictionalized voice can easily be mistaken for frivolity. But the scenes here—reflective of the push and pull of organizational life—should engage on an emotional level while offering more than one perspective.

In many ways, the preceding chapters used narrative fiction; that is, real data was provided, but certain details were woven in as reconstructed historical elements (Sparkes 2002). My book started with the story of Mitchy, a fictionalized character who is the embodiment of several women leaders. In retelling my participants' stories, I used their comments and added historical or cultural events to provide context and bring their experiences to life. Verbatim quotes came from interview notes, e-mail correspondence, and recorded meetings. Ms. Ali's story with the knife-wielding colleague is true—this horrific event did happen—but the early morning walk through the streets of Toronto did not. The scene illustrates the chilling gravity of the event. She was (accurately) described as walking arm in arm with her boyfriend (also true), which allows the reader to visualize the scene while maintaining her anonymity. Narrative fiction provides a creative way to address multiple topics and uncover organizational issues through the experiences of these women (Coffey and Atkinson 1996; Sparkes 2002; Trahar 2011).

The following short story—using a fictional voice and setting—is specifically written to draw readers into the experience on a visceral and emotional level (Speedy 2008). Adopting the writing style of Harlan Coben (2009, 2011) and Joseph Finder (2008) (two *New York Times* best-selling authors of murder mysteries), I attempted to use their style and the rhetorical use of questions to unravel events and uncover plots and personalities. Many mystery novels have a story line and characters unfold through punchy and purposeful dialogue in short chapters. A good mystery sets the scene and engages the reader by revealing a questionable action in the first few pages. I had noticed a particular pattern used by Joseph Finder and Harlan Coben. Finder actually outlines this structure on his website. Both writers use one- or two-word titles capturing the book's essence. For example, Finder's book *Power Play* (2008) is about a political power play at work that ends in murder. Coben's book *Tell No One* (2009) has the protagonist relive a horrific event from earlier years, and he is afraid to tell anyone. The books' chapters total no more than 1,400–1,500 words, and each chapter begins with a dialogue and within the first few sentences the reader is engaged, connected, and turns the pages quickly. I borrowed extensively from Coben's book *Live Wire* (2011) to develop the dialogue and created a similar title: "Dead Labels." The title is meaningful on two levels; it uses two words to follow the mystery genre and also links to Amy's organizational dilemma. The scene is fictitious, but the quotes are real, based on interviews, experiences, conversations, and events (Speedy 2008). I have rearranged sentences, reconfigured words, and used quotes, leaving deviations from correct grammar unchanged.

Our story begins in a conference room overlooking Victoria Harbor in Hong Kong.

~~~

"Dead Labels"
(With gratitude to Harlan Coben and Joseph Finder)

Difficult feedback, Ms. Lee stated, is healthier than a pocket full of platitudes. I thought about it, back to corporate America, where I'd ground it out for 18 years. Sugarcoated untruths cause heartache, destroy ideas, and so began a decade of lies, death of a career, a knife slowly inserted, twisted to ensure more pain. Gazing out of the large-paned glass window in Amy's office with thoughts of the blade going in the soft rib cage, I knew this was the last stop in her career.

Hunched over the terminal, her tears started. Got louder, convulsed into gasped sobs, the windows echoing back what was now a guttural groan. We stared at Amy's shaking silhouette at the desk, as she continued to look down at the floor, studying her shoes or the carpet. We remembered her first visit to the Hong Kong warehouse, that purposeful stride when she walked, the solid handshake and eye contact that caught you cold. Her presence was powerful. She'd reached the entire team, showing her tight grip on the organization. But that was all in the past, the warehouse seemed like decades ago. Nothing purposeful anymore. She'd been done in and sapped by an underhanded and unethical leader. She was the tough-as-nails negotiator who used to make everyone feel secure that they were on her side of the table. Only a shadow of that remained. She was now shaky, fragile even, under the constant power shifts at headquarters. Too much for even her to handle. Amy's face was strained, the stinging tears had reddened her usually creamy complexion, running mascara dripped down her sculpted cheekbones. It looked like a toxic spill. I guess it was.

Ms. Ali, Amy's colleague for over 12 years, sat in the conference room, shaking her head in disbelief. She haltingly looked our way, sloe-eyed, scared, appallingly vulnerable. A brilliant PhD, Ms. Ali was fiercely independent. Forever challenging ideas with sound intellect, keeping her staunch feminist views with a steely voice, she also had under her sari a favorite T-shirt she sometimes wore, "Educate Women, Educate a Generation."

Here she slouched with Ms. Ito, Ms. Lee, Ms. Chin, and me. Ms. Lee said "We're the A-team. We're all together because of our goals, drive to succeed, and far luckier than the vast majority of other women—and yet look at what happens when you are not watching." "Do you think God has a sense of humor?" she continued. "You mean Allah," said Ms. Ali.

No one replied.

"What does this situation tell us?" Ms. Ito asked both pensively and quietly.

Amy should have known better, and learned her lesson five years ago with the last leadership change. She revered her old boss, but it was not that simple. Corporate reality is a fool's paradise, devastating for naïve sycophants or overly driven "experts." That reality can smash a dream, stall careers, and stanch the flow of ideas—all the time. Amy never expected this, but she should have. The flashing lights had been there, but she looked the other way.

We moved to the conference room overlooking Hong Kong harbor, the thick humidity and the charred swirl of pollution blocking our view of Kowloon on the other side. Waiting for Amy, Ms. Lee fiddled with the blinds and called for tea. Within minutes Auntie

Chen entered the room, placing six delicate blue and white porcelain teacups on the table. She waited before pouring the fragrantly strong *pu-er cha,* the tea turning darker with each cup filled.

"*Mgoi sai,*" Ms. Chin and Ms. Lee whispered, tapping their forefingers on the table as Auntie poured and quietly left the room, bowing on her way out.

Placing her iPhone on the table, Ms. Chin leaned back, waved her hand, and nonchalantly said, "I have seen this happen, not surprising in big corporations."

"I am not really comfortable...," Ms. Ali replied, to no one in particular

Ms. Chin quickly interjected, "Some women just avoid politics and try to run away. Oh, but you can't, you know. You always get pulled in, like it or not." A trace of a smile, maybe not.

Ms. Ito stoically sat back and observed all around her, taking it all in, very sphinx-like.

"There is a lot more I would like to know...," Ms. Ali's voice trailed off.

Ms. Chin replied, "You are only as successful as your people if you don't give them recognition. It's a reflection of yourself. You won't move ahead otherwise."

Ms. Lee said, "Timely feedback has not been provided."

Amy burst into the room, eyes still down, cheeks flushed. She finally looked up and studied us all. "Just take a step back and just listen. No comments. Just listen. Please, everyone!" It was almost a shout, and we all collectively jumped a bit, silently looked at each other, collectively nodded.

Amy is not a damsel in distress, far from it. She was global head of consumer insights, had won major marketing campaigns for a competitive brand, made significant industry contributions. A known commodity herself, she was a player—expert in market research, viral marketing, consumer sentiment, and future trends; she'd also launched a "private label" product in China with significant revenue success. Private label was now the hot new idea inside the firm, thanks to her. So what happened?

Amy's boss was invited to the global sales and marketing conference to celebrate their success. He spoke at great length about "The great creativity of the Consumer Insight group" and positive return on investment. A colleague from another division attended the same meeting and said to Amy, "Hey, what happened? He didn't mention your name. Why not?" Amy brushed him off.

Three months later, Amy's boss was promoted. Not only promoted, but written up in the *Harvard Business Review* as an innovator for marketing and product innovation. Off the work she did.

Amy sits in his office, and being the direct woman she is, she asks him—tells him—about now wanting a promotion to VP. He shoots back acid "Work on your style and personal intensity, sweetheart." She may have been known for her detailed statistical analysis but not for interpersonal banter and style. So, after Amy delivers a billion dollars to the firm, she was passed over. And a flick of the wrist by her boss with a "Sorry, darlin', gotta do better."

Amy paused, and none of us spoke.

Ms. Lee leaned forward, placing perfectly manicured fingers on the mahogany conference table. "Expectations have not been communicated."

Ms. Ali: "What is the norm for recognition in this organization?"

Ms. Ito continued to quietly observe.

Amy turned to the group after a short while, aglow with renewed energy, like she was at the top of her game. "Two questions."

"What happened here?"

"What would you advise?"

"We're not asking the right questions," Ms. Ito said.

"She has a point," Ms. Ali said.

Facial expressions revealed conflicted emotions in our small group. Years ago, Amy trained herself to show little overlap between her personal and business life, but things had now changed. She pulled her Herman Miller chair over and forcefully sat down, almost bouncing up again.

Ms. Lee pointedly said, "Assumptions were made by you."

After this comment, Ms. Chin saw Amy's face sag, her sadness returned. Amy glanced around, then looked away, out the window to the haze. Ms. Chin bowed understandingly. She knew Ms. Lee was on to something.

Ms. Lee continued. "You should form strategic alliances with all the senior leaders' sponsorship—and always solicit their feedback, whether you like it or not."

Amy sighed, and then replied, "Perhaps we can find some way to better translate your comments, Lee. My boss has a huge ego." And then quickly added, "Is there any other kind? Who could imagine he'd do anything like this?"

"Amy, you need to understand how you are being perceived and what you must work on," Ms. Lee continued.

"Pardon?"

Ms. Lee, a firm believer in process, started to be more pointed. "What happened with your performance review dialogue?"

Ms. Ito looked around the room, her slight smile widening.

Ms. Ali stood up to stretch, walked over to the window to try and find any junks in the harbor, but after a squint through the darkened sky, she sat back down.

Ms. Lee interjected, "Performance appraisals led to her disappointment and regarding comments on her leadership capabilities."

Ms. Chin said, "I'm not sure. I think it's very much an individual thing."

Amy asked, "Have all of you seen this before—with women more than men?"

Ms. Chin remarked, "I feel that there's this thing called the gut feeling, a sixth sense women have."

Ms. Lee spoke directly to Amy, "Why don't you work with your coach to accelerate the development track and communicate progress?"

Turning to Ms. Chin, Amy asked her to continue about that sixth sense.

Ms. Chin replied, "The awareness with women is there, but whether they will do something about it is another story...they may shy away."

Ms. Lee responded, "You hadn't made your career objectives clear to your boss."

Ms. Chin was now thinking out loud, "I guess because I grew up in an American company I'm more assertive, more self-aware, and I dare to confront."

"As you move through the ranks you have more confidence," Ms. Lee said confidently.

Thinking about Ms. Lee's commentary, Amy turned now turned to Ms. Ali, "What would you advise?"

Ms. Ali was measured in her first reply. "Before I judge the boss's action or your feelings, I need to understand the norms. Without this kind of information, I think my responses would be based more on assumptions and prejudices rather than the situation per se."

There is no consensus.

Amy placed a brown confidential envelope on the table. The name on the envelope was Private Label China. The signature at the bottom of the report was Tim S., her boss. The name meant everything to the group. Amy's research was now owned by him, his bold capital letters, scrawled across the page.

Shocking.

Silence.

Absolutely.

"A Chinese chop sealed my fate," Amy said. Brushing aside her fringe, Amy turned to the group, "Do we ask the obvious question?"

Which is?

Ms. Chin said, "He stole your idea."

Can this really be happening?

The CEO believed the research was Tim's, that's all that matters.

"It does not appear to be morally right," Ms. Ali responded.

Amy moved around the conference room. Gone were the marketing campaigns and Chinese posters for the private label product. They had been taken down when Tim moved to corporate headquarters. Amy was not certain she wanted to see them ever again. Gone were the awards and the Veuve Cliquot champagne bottles from the celebratory events. Amy's Interbrand cover story, team photos, and marketer of the year award—gone, with one exception: the *China Daily* front cover, faded and yellowing, was left on the wall, with the tagline, "What comes next?" Amy thought and whispered to herself, "Resignation." Why anyone kept the *China Daily* photo on the wall she didn't know. Looking around the room, Amy realized how fleeting fame could be. You start your career believing everyone has the right intentions. You see the good in people—it's human nature. Her eyes began to tear up again. Her thoughts were now clouded by the discussion, and she remembered three things. One: be true to self; Two: do not hurt others; and Three: trust but verify. She spun around to notice Ms. Ito, still and silent, watching the game unfold.

~~~

Reflections on Fictional Dialogue

Good fiction slows our pace; we stop, visualize, reminisce, and anticipate next steps. Using a fictionalized setting interrupts and provokes thinking, providing time to peek behind curtains and see participants from a different angle, discussing a common workplace scenario. In this story everyone plays a role and is an active participant. The dialogue offers a glimpse inside organizations, adding individual dimensions to the study. In this particular scene, Ms. Chin and Ms. Lee have considerably stronger voices, correlating to their responses during the interviews. Ms. Lee's thoughts reflect her belief in organizational systems. Ms. Chin's comments demonstrate experiences aligned with the organizational culture where she works. Ms. Ali and Ms. Ito are noticeably less vocal but very much present. Ms. Ali's academic perspective comes through in her need for more information before responding. Ms. Ito shows how she observes the world, standing back to discover. Creating this story provided a way to visualize group dynamics and to experience organizational reality. There is a reflexive quality about this story; the reader draws on multiple sources of knowledge, looks back on actions, and draws from diverse experiences.

Reading or listening to a descriptive, evocative, or emotional tale draws us in. Soap operas, *telenovelas*, Korean dramas, Bollywood movies, or Mother Goose—we are all captivated by a good story. Fictionalized dialogue provides a platform to uncover a discussion that may have been overlooked or brushed aside, like whispered dialogue about "politics" often heard at work. Narrative fiction is not without critics. This way of writing research is hardly new; there are well-established, published works in psychotherapy and education using fiction, fictionalized voice, and storytelling methodology (Clough 2002; Speedy 2008; Trahar 2011). This creative method brings reflexivity to the forefront, exposing the researcher in the dialogic process and disclosing to the reader intricacies within the story, drawing on collective reflexivity, the participants' references, and the readers' perspective as it is triggered in the moment of reading.

The setting allows for the participants' voices to be heard equally and shows the reader differences between these voices and views (Trahar 2011). Using a standard format to present Amy's story, followed by a list of verbatim comments would not have the same impact nor allowed for the participant's personality to come through. This stiff format, similar to placing everyone in a petri dish, could not illustrate the multiplicity of dimensions or highlight individual voices. This fictionalized format pierces through personalities, jars our memory, and offers a scenic route rather than using flat, unemotional words.

In this story, the reader has a seat in the conference room to also ruminate and be part of an experience that impacts everyone. More important, the reader muses from a distance while paying attention to the peculiarity of the situation. The story recreates interviews and reshuffles content, but the words remain accurate. Ambling through the richness of the environment brings participants fully to life and draws on feelings that might not otherwise be apparent (Brown and Rhodes 2005). The story presents evidence, and using these facts the reader forms an opinion or suggests an action. At the same time, the story evokes emotions that challenge the reader about the situation, the participants, and their beliefs. It is through reframing and recognizing what we carry into this story that we can clarify our thinking about the situation and ultimately about workplace politics. The story provides the experience and reflexively allows us to look back on ourselves thus making learning possible.

This short scenario reconstructs an exploratory dialogue that brings workplace politics to the forefront. In many ways, this entire study could be written as a mystery to investigate the mysterious disappearance of women from decision-making roles (Coffman et al. 2010). This disappearance has been linked to organizational political maneuvering. Buchanan and Badham (2008) and Barsh (2011) suggest that office politics—or rather the aversion to politics—is one reason why women leave organizations in midcareer, resulting in underrepresentation at executive levels. Given the negative sentiments people have around politics and power, this might be the case.

The reality is that an organization is a political entity, and political skill is part of leadership. Instead of looking at the dark side of politics, the first step is to reframe thinking and consider a neutral standpoint to assess how politics, power, and organizations work.

Examining Politics

This fictional dialogue created a space to discuss workplace politics as a critical leadership skill with links to ethical behavior (Baddeley and James 1987; Brandon and Seldman 2004). For some, these two words—"politics" and "power"—are uncomfortable discussion topics. Mention the word "politics" and watch arms fold, eyebrows frown, and disgruntled comments ensue. Such reactions are remnants, detritus, left over from the industrial age of command and control management and overuse of power. Politics is part of the organizational fabric lining the hallways of the executive suite.

When researching workplace politics, Simon Baddeley, Kim James, and Tonya Arroba (1987, 2005) found two dimensions, "reading" and "carrying," critical for developing political skill and for leadership. The reading dimension provides an external perspective coupled with the carrying dimension, which is the internal reflection on what is carried into a situation, similar to seeing a glass as half empty or half full. The political innocent carries a naïve perspective and the adroit politician a discerning view. Whether innocent or skillful, those carrying a negative perspective bring a game-playing Machiavellian view of politics. Some organizational scholars consider "politics and politicking an essential aspect of organizational life and not necessarily an optional or dysfunctional extra" (Morgan 1997, 154). Bolman and Deal view politics and power through the lens of relationships, and at a basic level everyone needs an ally or sponsor to get things done, sell an idea, drive change, or complete a project. "It is hard to dislike politics without disliking people" (Bolman and Deal 2008, 220. Seldman and Brandon) define "organisational politics as an informal, unofficial, and sometimes behind-the-scenes efforts to sell ideas, influence an organisation, increase power, or achieve other targeted objectives" (2004, 2). Henry Mintzberg (1989, 2007), McGill University's management expert, views politics as a necessary evil, something to be learned but ultimately divisive. In this case, Mintzberg might be referring to Tim S., Amy's boss, the ambitious and self-centered politician with an oversized ego in "Dead Labels." There are two sides to Machiavelli, two sides to politics, and multiple definitions. Adding to Bolman and Deal's definition, and its Greek origins, politics is about building coalitions or relationships among diverse groups for the good of the state, organization, or team. How you read a situation and what you carry into the organization matters.

A strategy of ignoring relationships, not building networks, or not reading the organizational nuances is no strategy, but rather a high-priced mistake. As in the case of Amy, not embracing the political arena derailed what was a stellar career. We can see from the multiple definitions of politics that not everyone agrees with this line of thinking. According to Simon Baddeley and Kim James, "Political skill is the elusive and increasingly demanded ingredient of success and survival in organizational life" (1987, 3). Based on my experience in talent management, similar to Buchanan and Badham's observations, women who were passionately against "politics" were the same ones passed over for promotion. Too often the political innocent or maladroit managers, lacking this skill, fall off the talent ladder. At the same time, organizations continue to place emphasis on savvy skills when selecting leaders.

Most leadership competency frameworks highlight or reference political skills as an essential leadership competency. Daniel Goleman's work on emotional intelligence makes direct references to learning political savvy and leadership. Goleman states, "The ability to read political realities is vital to the behind-the-scenes networking and coalition building that allows someone to wield influence—no matter what their professional role. Mediocre performers lack such social acumen and so betray a distressingly low level of political savvy" (Goleman 1998, 160). If only the savvy survive, then organizations need to level the playing field and develop political skills throughout the company. Examining the definition of politics helps in reframing our thinking about organizational life. The ability to read the organizational subtleties and navigate informal networks strengthens the emotional intelligence needed for leadership. To build this skill requires development in political savvy from an organizational systems perspective. This development should begin at universities and on the first day on the job.

There is ample research exploring women's disinclination to embrace the political arena across many cultures, not only in Asia (Rhode 2003; Wilson 2007). McKinsey uncovered "politics" as one of the reasons for high attrition and lower promotions among women (Barsh and Yee 2011). This provides one explanation for the absence of women from the executive suites. Other researchers believe a lack of access to power or the fact that "women are less likely to engage in, or make use of, organizational politics, preferring instead to rely on formal means to advance up the executive ladder" (Buchanan and Badham 2008, 154). This is not necessarily so; women have access to power, and many are connected to power through sponsors and connected networks. In my study, my participants' web of inclusion ensured connections to powerful networks. Some researchers indicated the stress linked with managing workplace politics coupled with juggling multiple roles could have been the reason for midcareer turnover. Rather than a reluctance to embrace political savvy, women may not see the links to leadership. Perrewe and Nelson (2004) indicate "women tend to view career success as linked with task accomplishments and expertise. They believe if their work is good enough, and they are competent enough, they should be rewarded (promoted) in organizations" (2004, 371). Too often in talent discussion with executives the focus is on "visibility" and "networks" with questions such as, "who knows this person or what do they do?" These questions can be career limiting, particularly if the business leader is asking. On the other hand, the politically savvy mangers are well-known, recognized favorably, and networked broadly, which places them higher on the talent ladder. Savvy leaders demonstrate strong interpersonal influence skills and ultimately increase their value to the organization. Research conducted among managers in China positively links savvy ability and increased power to career progression and promotions (Liu et al. 2010). Understandably then, the politically unaware emerging leader is often overlooked or placed on the "needs development" talent plan.

While competency frameworks highlight political awareness, political savvy, or political agility as leadership skills and use these same frameworks to evaluate future talent, few organizations teach this skill. When talent is placed on "needs development," the plan does not match the individuals' needs. This links back to how organizations "read" politics. The bottom line is that workplace politics must be developed across the organization in order to level the playing field and ensure the right leaders move ahead.

Last year I was approached by the publishing firm John Wiley and Sons to write a business self-help book on organizational politics. The book, *I Wish I'd Known That Earlier in My Career: The Power of Positive Workplace Politics* (2012), examines cross-cultural and gender aspects of workplace politics. As seen in the research, the topic of politics is not new; as with leadership, volumes have been written on this subject. Yet, combining workplace politics and unconscious bias provide two strong obstacles keeping women from reaching their full potential (Barsh and Yee 2010; Eagly 2007; Wilson 2007; Buchanan and Badham 2008; Perrewe and Nelson 2004). Surrounded by politics, some women consider that "hard work and head down" ensures success and makes politics go away. In reflections on Amy's plight, these same sentiments became apparent. Politics and politicking are part and parcel of organizational life, not necessarily self-serving but a natural outcome of having to manage competing interests and resources.

Politics are everywhere and very much alive in all work settings. Some researchers suggest "women are less likely to engage in, or make use of, organisational politics, preferring instead to rely on formal means to advance up the executive ladder" (Buchanan and Badham 2008, 154). Yet, can we say categorically that women avoid politics? I would argue, and research supports my view, that women have the intuitive attributes and communal skills necessary for political savvy. Rather than avoiding politics, women embrace savvy differently and are therefore misunderstood or misinterpreted. Underlying savvy (and leadership) is the ability to influence others toward a shared goal. Comparing influence strategies between men and women, women with preference for soft power lean toward coalition building and working across diverse groups. Having a natural proclivity toward building coalitions seems relevant for contemporary organizations and appropriate for twenty-first-century leaders. Admittedly, there are stereotypes contrasting men and women across the gamut of political savvy skills. Calling out the differences in influence tactics falls under this bias. Looking at political savvy across cultures, savvy skills reflect the individuals' preference adapted to the different groups and situations (Liu et al. 2010). In this particular fictitious dialogue session, the story highlights the ingrained socialization the women received from their particular organizations. Ms. Chin's and Ms. Lee's responses reflected not only cultural values but years of experience in multinational organizations. As with savvy, there are individual differences in leadership, and situational context matters more than culture or gender.

Baddeley and James (1987) developed a political model of behavior, based on animals, to discuss politically aware and unaware leaders. Their animal scale is as follows: owl, donkey, sheep, and fox, and it elicits chuckles from some, but the important point is the internal intuitive and external perspective that is carried into situations. Assumptions and perceptions define reactions and how an organization is read. A political savvy leader, instead of using self-serving tactics, displays an acute awareness of organizational context and focuses on influencing followers for the good of the organization or team (Ammeter et al. 2002). Reflecting on this notion of reading and carrying, we see that the same mind-set is needed regarding narrative inquiry. I brought a Western educational view on organizations and leadership to this inquiry, but based on my years of global experience I read situations differently. Sometimes I carried a cynical view, recoiling from "management-speak" which is not usually aligned with my thinking. As seen with workplace politics, sometimes a situation can be viewed too narrowly or negatively.

Concluding Thoughts

This corporate fable was written to grab attention, share subtle nuances, and highlight challenges women face in organizations. Like a movie using imaginary scenes and rich dialogue, this easy-to-read story is intended to make readers pause, consider, and offer new perspectives on an ordinary event (Spindler 2008). It reinforces the value of reflexivity, of taking a step back, of being critically self-aware, and of evaluate what we carry into a story. The format offered a different perspective on the participants to learn from their collective experiences, and it addresses organizational politics from a multicultural and female perspective. Understandably, using fiction is difficult and can be mistaken for frivolity (Speedy 2008), but this scene from organizational life jolts the readers' memory of similar events. Creating fictitious scenes, playing a role, mimicking writing styles, all bring together voices and viewpoints. This story (in the middle of a study) should not be misconstrued as lacking rigor (Speedy 2008). Instead, this chapter surfaces issues of intellectual dissonance for a discussion on workplace politics using the creative process of narrative fiction. The intention is to encourage the reader to use reflexivity and to take a step back before making any judgment, as I have done many times in this project.

CHAPTER 7

Unconscious Bias Uncovered

In this chapter I enter unchartered ground, the slippery slope of discussing unconscious bias. I have several reasons for writing this chapter on bias. I first uncovered unconscious bias when conducting narrative interviews. Equipped with a multicultural mindset, I was struck by this quiet deception. I have also observed and witnessed unconscious bias operating across organizations, impacting efforts at diversity and inclusion, specifically for women. In addition, unconscious bias is considered one of the barriers keeping women from achieving leadership positions (Barsh and Yee 2011; Barsh et al. 2012; Eagly and Mladinic 1995). Since this study captures lessons of experience, bias played a role in understanding and must be discussed and confronted.

The mere mention of bias produces confused looks—like the concepts politics and power, bias generates a visceral reaction, one immediately filed under "negative." I define bias as a tendency, conscious or unconscious, that hinders one's ability to see or accept something new or different, unlike positivist hard science that controls for bias. Bias is our natural proclivity to choose one thing over another, and it is *not* always negative. Bias triggers an automatic reaction toward a person, place, or thing. I witnessed rushed decisions and automatic judgments at work as well as an overreliance on one specific quality in selecting people to leadership positions.

Based on my experience in multinational organizations, I would wager that two of the four women in this study might not be considered for leadership positions, but all four possess leadership abilities. An organization may not see their accomplishments even though all four women are extremely capable. One reason could be that leadership theory is not clearly defined and skewed toward masculine characteristics (Eagly 2007; Ciulla 2004; Chin et al. 2007; Tarr-Whelan 2009). In addition, entrenched beliefs or unconscious bias of what constitutes leadership remain buried within organizational beliefs. Working in a multicultural environment adds to the complexity—and richness. This incongruent phenomenon—bias— carries us through daily life, impacts organizational systems, and frequently jumbled my thoughts. In this chapter, I explore bias in cross-cultural narrative and evaluate the impact on women within organizations. I will share examples of instances when my unconscious mind both fooled and troubled me during interviews and when writing stories.

Cultural Beliefs or Bias in Narrative Inquiry

Combing through narrative research, specifically cross-cultural narrative inquiry, I found references and discussions on bias in narrative (Phillion 2002; He 2002; Mitchell 2012; Stivers 1993; Larson 1997). Ming Feng He (2002) made assumptions and grappled with notions of bias, illusions, and complexities within cultural definitions. I also entered this research thinking culture was the least of my concerns, and like Phillion, faced my own challenges. Research begins with broad experiences, intellectual pursuits, and often bookish assumptions. There is no doubt such ingrained knowledge and entrenched beliefs, tucked away in the recesses of our minds, affect our perspective. How could they not? Instead of setting me free, my cross-cultural knowledge trapped me and obscured my thinking. The word "culture" has become tainted and is sometimes misaligned with life (He 2002). Rather than blaming the definition of culture, I realized my mistake; I applied my cultural definitions too broadly and adhered to my cultural ideals too rigidly. The concept of culture is not the issue; the challenge is to deal with unconscious elements we all carry with us.

Narrative research brings an understanding of our self, our standpoint, our lived experiences, and our knowledge. Phillion carried "her cherished beliefs" (Clandinin and Connelly 2000, 44) into multicultural narrative at the Bay Street School. I brought years of cross-cultural experience and knowledge from many Asian cultures to my study. In both situations this knowledge caused discomfort, with the potential of obstructing acceptance of differences. I assumed my cross-cultural knowledge provided a broader perspective even though I knew the limitations. I first thought the cultural construct of family applied across cultures. Unconsciously applying this universal ideal became deeply troubling, and I was soon faced with the same insularity and rigid thinking which I'd admonished others for when working in organizations.

I uncovered this dilemma during interviews and while developing narratives. Disappointed with myself, I wanted to see if others had faced similar challenges. Phillion's emotionally expressive story on Koto to Pan story, reminiscing about the fluidity of culture, revealed to her "the role of bias in narrative inquiry" (Phillion 2002, 547) complexities of instinct and detachment. I appreciated Phillion's comment that "until I understood how my biases (together with theory) could be impediments to understanding classroom life, [I] was limited in what I could understand" (Phillion 2002, 538). I also held on to my preconceived notion of Asian values, blindly applying a Western leadership framework from the work of James McGregor Burns (2010) and Howard Gardner (1995), which distracted my interviews and confused my writing. Based on Gardner's global leadership study, I assumed "failure" and "resilience" were defined and understood the same way across cultures, but discovered the choice of words made a great difference.

Caught in the fog of cross-cultural sensitivity, I could not separate the individual from the story. This inability to see the individual could be the "difference between thinking narratively and thinking formalistically" (Clandinin and Connelly 2000, 45), or could be attributed to the researcher's naiveté. As much as I tried to move away from theory, I unconsciously became a captive of my idea of a multicultural framework. I would argue that unconscious bias is embedded deep within cognitive processes which structure narrative. I also assert this is one of the organizational challenges for the selection of leadership positions.

At a particularly low point while conducting interviews, I struggled with participant responses—reading back over my notes was a boring walk into overly familiar terrain. I had entered unknown territory and began to question what I was doing and where this was headed. Feeling impaired, I realized my participants were not representative of culture or gender, nor bound by any such restrictions I might have placed on them. I managed myself through these events by understanding the value of reflexivity and becoming consciously aware of bias. Thinking reflexively, I started to see my world—and theirs—from a different vantage point. Reflexivity plays an important role in this narrative, but should also be considered part of an organizational curriculum. Socrates advised knowing one's self before understanding others. Confucius counseled reexamining one's self when "the other" acts out of character; both wise maxims to apply.

Personal Struggles with Bias

For those who may think they're not biased, the nature of deception is such that one never knows when being deceived, especially by oneself. I discovered my own unconscious bias, finding myself blocked by the very knowledge in which I had placed my trust. On the one hand, I operated from an understanding of myself as a culturally cognizant Ms. Multicultural (Phillion 2002). On the other hand, I functioned from a cultural bias, which became apparent when I asked questions. The word "failure," for example, stalled the discussions, resulting in long silences or blank expressions. Silence is often unnerving and unsettling in conversations, but I sat comfortably during prolonged pauses. When participants answered my questions with a nontraditional response which was unexpected, I was struck by my discomfort, a resistance to see things differently. For example, when Ms. Ito responded to my question about early childhood influences flatly stating there had been no one, her unexpected answer stunned me. Looking through my notes, I remember going back to Ms. Ito to ask the same question from a different angle. This was the same behavior I saw with culturally maladroit executives at work and witnessed with customs officials at airports—to wit, assuming that by repeating the same question more slowly or loudly we will somehow get the response we want to hear.

Ms. Ito's lack of response and my reflection on the incident gave me pause for thought. I had difficulty accepting her reaction and realized that this is common in feminist and cross-cultural narrative inquiry; we tend to make broad assumptions and reflections throughout cultures (Visweswaran 1994). The struggle is not only cultural; feminist researchers refrain from applying a set of attributes for all women while not denying shared qualities (Reinharz and Chase 2001). Examining feminist ethnographers, I assumed there were consistencies or similarities among women in different cultures (Reinharz 1992). In my professional work, this is often referred to as unconscious bias or stereotyping. Taking time to reflect on this setback, I became painfully aware of my blind spots. I changed questions in an attempt to bring an open mind to the task an empathetic understanding and external perspective on culture and gender which might be beneficial (Gorelick 1991). As I started writing this study, I rediscovered the difficulty of trying to set aside my knowledge, culture, values, and beliefs. My reaction to Ms. Ito's response was based on naiveté, bias, or control. In hindsight, I wanted the response to this innocent question to follow my format. While I attempted to be open to the complexities of the situation, I was often unable to move beyond my frame of reference. More alarming, I was struck by both my resistance and emotions.

Some responses fit my understanding of cultures influenced by Confucianism, yet others clearly did not (Spence 1990; Fairbank 1992). From a feminist position, I believed Asian women had a special type of knowledge, different from everyone else's (Hirschman 1997; Harstock 2004). Reflecting on my reactions, I began reading more feminist research and issues of bringing the self into the research process. Feminist interviewing does not exclusively lead to understanding or correcting an interpretation (Reinharz 1992). There were times when I rejected input from my participants. For example, when they sounded too agreeable, cloying, or had used stilted language. When this occurred, I wrote a comment in my notebook to review the response later. On some occasions I put the interview aside and challenged myself to understand the participants in their "own terms and not from a particular social context" (Reinharz 1992, 26). The stories I created are multifaceted bringing together my memories and their insights providing multiple avenues and ways of experiencing different perspectives, not as singular isolated events but as part of a continuum (Hamdan 2009). I did strive to maintain a balance of voice, as my aim was to appreciate the individual. After all, individuality is what made all my participants leaders. Interestingly, I exhibited the same bias I experienced in organizations, creating a mental barrier for the person in front of me—the same invisible barrier which holds women back from the executive suite. Alarmingly, I had uncovered my lofty attitude; I thought I acted from a position of multicultural awareness, but assumed everyone else was incapable of doing so.

Organizational Fixedness

The ubiquitous unconscious nature of bias could be one factor affecting women's rise to leadership positions. Joanna Barsh and Lareina Yee (2011) and Alice Eagly (2007) believe bias is one reason for women's slow entry into the executive suite and into decision-making roles. With all the awareness of the lack of women in the boardrooms, why does this still happen? I discovered that in research many academics and professionals discussed bias and barriers for women (Barsh and Yee 2011; Eagly 2007; Coughlin et al. 2005; Ely et al. 2011). McKinsey (Barsh, Cranston, and Craske 2008) believes entrenched mindsets hinder women, and Eagly (2007) cites evidence of discrimination for women navigating the labyrinth of organizations. Although I did not ask about bias or the glass ceiling, Ms. Chin refuted the notion of a glass ceiling at her company. She understood the challenges for some women to balance life and work, particularly for young mothers, but believed her organization offered many opportunities for both men and women to advance. However, as the head of organizational development, I could see these barriers were entrenched deeply in organizational systems, particularly for leadership positions.

Biased Leadership Selection

Leadership selection highlights the challenges bias presents with its implicit associations and misplaced ideas around physical attributes, communication styles, and other loosely defined qualities. Leadership carries a bias regarding physical dimensions. For example, less than 15 percent of American men are over six foot tall (1.8 meters), yet almost 60 percent of corporate CEOs are over six feet tall (Ross 2008). Based on my work experience, I have seen similar unconscious connections equating height with leadership. In addition to height, names present another set of challenges (Ross 2008). Consulting with a European bank, one hiring manager mentioned that undecipherable names are tossed aside, ensuring an interviewer is not embarrassed by any mispronunciation. Assumptions or perceptions made early on in a career, either through talent management or performance appraisals, influencing decisions about promotions or demotions. Ultimately, these assumptions have potential to impact on who is viewed as a future leader. Eagly and Carli (2007) recommend improving the performance review process to reduce the rater's bias by clarifying criteria for development and promotions.

In Asia challenges regarding bias can be seen with accents—for example, working with an investment bank in talent selection, a top woman executive in wealth management was put on the "needs development" track to improve her English language skills. She was serving wealthy clients in China, where the lingua franca was Mandarin.

English is the global language of business, which means everyone speaks with an accent. So, who owns the accent or which accent is preferred? The top three languages based on the number of people speaking them are Mandarin, Hindi, and Spanish. English ranks fourth. Over the next decade, Arabic could possibly take fourth place. In multicultural work environments the majority of the workforce speaks languages that are not their native tongue. Proficiency in multiple languages benefits global organizations; it seems patently unfair and absurd to draw conclusions on leadership based on accents, yet these decisions may continue unless bias is checked and challenged.

Gender Bias and Word Choices

Gender associations attached to leadership, specifically perceptions of achievement and ambition, highlight some of the challenges posed by bias. Wilson (2007) found that men are expected to be ambitious achievers, but this same trait elicits negative labels in women. Viewed as nurturers, achievement-oriented female executives sometimes struggle when acting outside of the 'caring' role (Wilson 2007; Eagly 2007). These associations impact leadership potential by attaching value to different skills and contributions (Kolb and McGuinn 2009). There appears to be confusion around word meanings and assumptions concerning leadership. The misinterpretation of words, specifically ambition, may be one of the challenges in certain cultures. When I asked my participants about failure, the term did not register. Can we thus assume that ambition equates with leadership? Maybe so, and maybe not. The choice of words surrounding or defining leadership carries different cultural meanings.

For example, examining the word "ambition" from a North American perspective, Wilson (2007) discovered that ambitious women were negatively labeled and made pariahs for exhibiting such behavior. More recently, women have been criticized for not displaying or having ambition (Waldman 2012; Ettus 2012). The term is perplexing in Asia. Hewlett and Rashid (2011) found that 75 percent of women in China and India had aspirations for top positions, and thus one would assume this group is comfortable with the word "ambition." I rarely heard participants use this word; they were more comfortable discussing contributions rather than ambition. In Vietnam and Korea, I discovered this term connotes a combination of evil and greed. It is not a label anyone wants, particularly in Vietnam, which has had several corruption scandals recently. When working in multicultural work environments, it is important to recognize the impact of word choices. Likewise, it is also important to accept that leadership definitions vary greatly. Organizations need to have a flexible mindset and be open to differences, just as I discovered individuality more sharply, and learned to appreciate it more thoroughly.

Another stumbling block I uncovered in leadership selection was the overemphasis on one quality, not necessarily a competency or trait. In talent meetings, I often saw Asian women overlooked for promotions because of a perceived lack of presence; they were not considered visible enough. Breaking down the meaning of "presence" is problematic, due to its subjective nature and cultural overtones. Presence is sometimes linked to charisma, but how is charisma depicted across cultures? A charismatic leader in Beijing might display behaviors different from one in Boston, Mumbai, or Buenos Aires. Ms. Ito with her deep *saikeiri* bow, her humble nature, and quietly observant demeanor might not be considered charismatic or having presence. Yet I believe her to be a leader with a track record of success.

While the Global Leadership and Organizational Behavior Effectiveness (GLOBE) study (House et al. 2004) on cross-cultural leadership positively maps charismatic leadership across multiple Asian cultures, specifically Taiwan and Japan, I found the behaviors to be different. We need to accept others rather than label them. In the same manner, we should not "see someone from Taiwan" and make a general statement on behavior. Reflecting on Ms. Lee's story, I see this as one reason for her fall from grace. The sequence of events in her story show Ms. Lee spent the bulk of her career in South Africa working with many African cultures and tribes as the only woman on the senior management team. She relocated to Hong Kong, armed with an advanced business degree and a decade of experience leading diverse teams, and met unfamiliar challenges. I suspect it was an incongruent style, hers being a direct "tell it like it is" communicator and asking challenging questions, which caught others off guard and resulted in her becoming a pariah within the organization. Women of Asian heritage are often categorized as less ambitious and quieter, placing them in a precarious position (Ely et al. 2011). If they act outside of this stereotype—as Ms. Lee did—they are likely to be categorized and brought down. This bias on what leadership (should) look like, how someone from one culture should behave is reinforced, and can [wrongly] influence the decision makers.

In some cases leaders with a gift for speaking openly and candidly may move ahead of others. Yet, I have also observed the visible and vocal ones overshadowed by an observant, humble leader. Animated qualities can easily be mistaken for charisma (Kouzes and Posner 2002). In hindsight, as I sat in talent management meetings,

I wished for the courage to challenge promotion decisions and question the prevailing thinking on leadership. However, challenging decisions with those in a position of power requires courage and self-awareness to step back and reflect and pay close attention to the moment. This awareness keeps us on track, allows our conscience to be our guide, aware of what we cannot immediately grasp, and ultimately exposes our limiting beliefs and unconscious bias (Shope 2006). This self-examination became apparent, particularly in the narratives of Ms. Ito, Ms. Ali, and Ms. Lee. Reflexivity played an important role, providing insights many times throughout this research journey, specifically uncovering personal bias. In my opinion, reflexivity, turning inward and being self-aware, with a dash of courage, should be part of an organization's process in selecting candidates for leadership positions in multicultural, gendered environments.

Building Inclusive Organizations

Men and women are viewed differently regarding leadership competencies, categories, or attributes (Wilson 2007; Eagly and Mladinic 1995; Heifetz 2007). As recently as 2006, a *New York Times* article headline asked, "Hillary can run but can she win?" (Herbert 2006) The article did not question Hillary's capability as a hard-working and extremely intelligent person; the focus was primarily on her gender. While many women like Clinton have the "right stuff" for leadership, they are usually not selected for senior positions. Bain Consulting called this phenomenon "the great disappearing act" (Coffman et al. 2010, 1). Recently some remedies have been tried to build an inclusive work environment and solve the gender problem; most place emphasis on leadership development for women only. This focus assumes a women's problem exclusively (Ely et al. 2011). Instead of creating programs to fix the *women,* a better approach would be to redefine and accept different styles of leadership.

Bias can also be experienced in the selection process and can be exacerbated in hierarchical and traditional organizational cultures. Men are viewed positively for authoritative traits and behavior—or what Eagly (2007) has labeled an agentic leadership style—while women are labeled negatively when using this same style. Likewise, direct and candid communication is acceptable for male leaders but labeled aggressive in women (Tannen 2001; Buchanan and Badham 2008; Wilson 2007). Cross-cultural settings may inflame this situation, and Ms. Lee's story highlights such challenges. In my experience, Asian women are viewed as humble, quiet, and unassertive. If they engage in direct, candid communication, this raises a red flag or initiates calls to an executive coach for remedying. It is no wonder that women have difficulty navigating this organizational maze and often overlooked (Eagly and Carli 2007; Wilson 2007). As I examined leadership competency frameworks and the definition of leadership, I found most are skewed toward the Western and male profile (Ciulla 2004; Eagly 2007). In addition to these frameworks, followers or managers with aspirations mimic the prevailing style in organizations. "Women leaders more commonly lead in the context of a male advantage, that is, masculinized contexts; they are evaluated and perceived differently from men based on our current gender-related biases" (Chin et al. 2007, 357). Therefore, they experience the brunt of bias on career advancement.

Asia presents a unique set of challenges due to cultural norms, a traditional expectation for women to marry young and raise children (Francesco and Mahtani 2011; Swenson 2009). In my research, I found those perceived challenges became opportunities for my participants, as they had successfully integrated family, tradition, and career. The real issue of untested assumptions and unconscious bias from North American and European managers remains unchallenged—that is, the belief that all Asians are humble, quiet, and reserved. Worse, these values are often applied equally to women across cultures. During my interviews, I found myself stuck in the murky waters of unconscious bias and cultural generalizations, putting Asians into one category and assuming traditional formalities were critical for support. When participants responded otherwise, it took time before I accepted their answers. I cannot blame cultural ignorance for my reactions; the problem was more likely a sweeping generalization. In my opinion and experience, the same holds true for organizations.

Time to Change

Despite increasing numbers of women in the workforce, old beliefs and views on leadership have not dissipated. The global workforce continues to change, but many organizational mindsets are a step behind, despite laws stipulating inclusion in North America, the United Kingdom, Europe, and parts of Asia (Kandola 2009). Demographic statistics now show women entering the workforce at the same rate as men, and more often with advanced degrees and academic authority (Hewlett 2007). In the hallowed hallways and echelons of executive suites, too few women are found. While recognized for leadership excellence, many women are often in second place or mired in middle management, unable to move into leadership roles. In multicultural work environments, cultural norms can be unfairly skewed by a Western leadership perspective that compares women to men globally in terms of competency and social significance (Ridgeway 2011). Herbert's article on Hillary Clinton points to the problem: a mismatch between perceptions and the realities of a woman's role in society.

We can never eliminate bias, so how do we work with it? Moving forward, a better way to ensure a gender balanced and culturally diverse talent slate is to create a process where everyone is judged on the same criteria and nothing else. John Rawls, an American political philosopher, provides a new view on justice and equality. Rawls provocatively asks, "Suppose we gathered, just as we are, to choose principles to govern our collective life—to write a social contract. What principles would we choose?" (Sandel 2007, 141). Organizations following Rawls should use similar questions to reposition equality and inclusiveness in processes of leadership selection and promotion. They should take time before the selection process to determine principles and values of leadership needed to guide the organization into the future. One method is using a "blind veil" to conduct reviews when evaluating talent on leadership values and stripping away the physical attributes, perceptions, and emotions. Similar to Rawls's "veil of ignorance," this device would allow the organization to first determine what constitutes fairness and place everyone on the same level (Sandel 2007). Rawls's "veil of ignorance" presents a reasonable approach, clarifying the diversity arguments, boardroom discussions, and providing opportunities for change.

The next step is to take time to reflect and build reflexive thinking into organizational processes. Courage is very much a part of this process. In conducting this research, I had the courage to challenge myself, but that is very different from challenging powerful decision makers inside organizations. This continuous struggle with ways of knowing requires a reflexive turn inward; organizations should learn to do the same. Coming to the end of this chapter and in writing these stories, I realize the complexity and interweaving of relationships between my participants and myself. In the course of this journey I have been able to reflexively turn back on myself and the situation on numerous occasions (Davies 1999). In doing so, my bias became apparent, and my stories presented a new view. This reflexive turn is part of my narrative journey and integral to qualitative research (Dyck et al. 1995), but it is not necessarily a part of organizational life.

Concluding Thoughts

This reflexive turning inward is not easy for the neophyte researcher or an organizational leader. Inside organizations, can we truly distance ourselves from ingrained beliefs? The puzzle of bias is complicated by the unconscious element, rarely discussed, and therefore not easily resolved at work. Leadership selection is complicated by a biased decision-making process and ambiguous definitions of leadership for women (Bowles and McGuinn 2005). Instead of narrowly focusing on developing hi-potential talent, organizations should mandate the practice of reflexivity across all people processes to ensure they have not overlooked potential candidates. The corporate ability to pause and reflect in a manner that develops deep self-awareness is an important component of leadership—one that is still sorely lacking in many organizations (Coughlin et al. 2005).

CHAPTER 8

Leadership Review

L eadership can be a messy concept. James McGregor Burns called it the "most observed and least understood phenomena on earth" (2010, 2). Management books add to the confusion, redefining leadership while obscuring the concept. Researched widely and discussed broadly, there is surprisingly little consensus on definition. Complicating the question, much of the research emanates from the West, which is largely skewed toward the masculine, and embedded within competency models and organizational mind-sets (Ciulla 2004; Eagly 2007). The changes in today's organizations, fast-paced technology, globalization, and shifting demographics add to the fray. It is hard to believe the concept and clarification of "leadership" can both impact and determine careers. But it does.

The first decade of the twenty-first century highlighted leadership challenges. Beginning with the 9/11 terrorist attacks, the decade was later marked by a global financial crisis that struck a hard blow to leadership confidence and trust in organizations "too big to fail." However, some of the giants did indeed fail. Pensions blew up. Icons of business collapsed. Bear Sterns and Lehman Brothers closed. The US government's TARP program purchased over $40 billion worth of stock from Citibank, Bank of America, and AIG each, and over $10 billion apiece from JP MorganChase, Wells Fargo, Morgan Stanley, Goldman Sachs, and General Motors. All done in order for them to stay afloat.

The culture of greed left a large swath of disarray for individuals and governments around the world. In addition to these cataclysmic events, the workplace has fundamentally changed. Financial upheaval is now complicated by globally connected, multigenerational, multicultural, and mobile 24/7 workers. Global demographic shifts and increased talent mobility in the workforce are seismic, and such disruptions will continue for many years to come. Leadership is never easy, but the past decade and the present one have been a continuous roller-coaster ride, with no end in sight. A Chinese proverb reminds us that "every crisis brings opportunities" and amidst the turmoil emerging markets benefited. As financial storms raged in the West, opportunity rained across Asia, as MNC's shifted their focus eastward, more foreign direct investments poured in to emerging markets in Asia, and the Chinese yuan remains not fully convertible. This economic pivot bodes well for the Asia Pacific region, but the mistrust of organizational leadership and veracity remains. In order to gain long term benefits, a reframing and reevaluation of leadership and leaders is now required, a better definition that should include not only a more global perspective but more fully incorporate women as well.

I conducted a cross-cultural inquiry with four women in various stages of leadership, providing insights into what a different type of leadership looks like and how it works across cultures. My interviews were based on transformational leadership, using the work of James McGregor Burns, Bernard Bass, and Alice Eagly. While some scholars have queried the global application of American-centric definitions of leadership, transformational leadership has been tested across cultures, with positive correlations reported in Singapore and China (Jung and Avolio 1999; Dorfman et al. 1997; Fu et al. 2008; Koh et al. 1996).

Throughout this book, I openly discuss personal and organizational challenges using a Western framework, but in further research

I find links to both Confucianism and women (Eagly 2007; Bass and Steidlmeier 2004; Fu et al. 2008). Alice Eagly's extensive gender research indicates that while transformational leadership is androgynous, the communal coaching style of transformational leadership leans toward the feminine (2007). Burns suggests similar, ubiquitous practices across leadership globally. It is thus quite reasonable to assume that transformational leadership is grounded in ethics, authenticity, and legitimacy across all cultures.

I also discuss McKinsey's (Barsh et al. 2008) concept of centered leadership, Sally Helgesen's (1995) web of inclusion, and Cheung and Halpern's (2010) cross-cultural analysis of women executives. Through my interviews, I found similarities and connections to these studies. This chapter weaves my participants' stories into the discussion, uncovering the "how" of Asian women leaders who build inclusive webs and integrate family and work while remaining true to their values.

Transformational Leadership

Transformational leadership with an ethical foundation fills this void by providing a "moral environment for the organization" (Ciulla 2004, 184). Interestingly, women with a natural proclivity for transformational leadership have a slight advantage over men in this regard (Eagly 2007). The one quality that stood out was *individualized consideration,* or the ability to tap into individual motivations and engage a group of loyal followers. Grounded in a moral setting, global transformational leadership is linked to Asia, specifically Confucianism. Confucian philosophy searches for the greater good in humanity and strives to guide people to live a moral life. Confucianism holds that the "superior" person has a higher level of status and knowledge gained through education and self-awareness. For example, a father holds the superior position, and his sons are raised to follow this autocratic rule (Fairbank 1992). This type of hierarchy can offer insights into the challenges for women in Confucianism and into the more restrictive traditions affecting them within Asia. In particular, classic Confucian texts reinforce hierarchy and domination, specifically "parents over their children and husbands over their wives" (Spence 1990, 60). There is a surfeit of research on the restrictive cultural challenges Asian women face as they try to balance a career and family traditions (Tuminez 2012; Francesco and Mahtani 2011; Fleschenberg 2009; Ko et al. 2003). However, times change; a different picture is now emerging. The gender topic has been recast from a humane condition to an economic imperative by the prime ministers in Japan, Malaysia, and Bangladesh, articulating actions to retain women in the workforce for a nation's growth and stability.

Transformational and Transactional Leadership

Transformational leaders are moral role models working collaboratively toward common goals for the greater good (Ciulla 2004; Eagly 2007; Knapp 2007). These two words, "engage" and "exchange," illustrate the stark difference in leadership styles. A transformational leader moves well beyond short-term stratagems and understanding motivation to engage the whole person and hence organization in the pursuit of shared goals. This collective positioning illustrates the inclusive nature of transformational leadership, appropriately aligned with globally diverse organizations.

In contrast, transactional leadership emphasizes a performance exchange, a task-driven style based on the expectation of an annual reward. A transformational leader, however, works toward mutual benefit and collaborative goals; transactional leaders, on the other hand, separate the objectives of the leader from those of the followers (Ciulla 2004). Transactional leadership is actually misnamed; it should be renamed simply as management, of which the authority remains in a command and control style, as outlined in Frederick Taylor's scientific management theory prevalent during the first half of the twentieth century (Conger 1999; Morgan 1997). Taylorism focused on precision, keeping time, and training and is still used in manufacturing, fast-food restaurants, and retail and distribution environments. Frederick Taylor had a significant impact and influence on work systems, but he also became the most maligned organizational theorist (Morgan 1997).

The world of work now requires a different style of leadership, one that concentrates on collaboration to achieve collective goals for the good of the organization and society (Ciulla 2004). Unlike transactional management, transformational leadership requires leaders to engender trust and drive change through a common purpose shared with their followers (Ciulla 2004). Some scholars combine charisma with transformational leadership, but there are liabilities and inconsistencies in doing so (Conger 1999; Ciulla 2004). The baggage left over from the financial crisis illustrates the dark side of a charismatic leader. Charisma is often linked with presence and communication style. A humble, observant leader may be captivating in one culture and fall flat in another, and vice versa. Examining transformational leadership, Eagly (2007) highlighted the following five qualities: (1) and (2) idealized influence (behavior and attribute), (3) inspirational motivation, (4) intellectual stimulation, and (5) individualized consideration (as cited in Eagly et al. 2003; Ciulla 2004). Eagly and her colleagues found in their meta-analysis that women leaders were "more transformational than male leaders" (Eagly et al. 2003, 586). Women scored higher than men on aligning motivation, using rewards, and encouraging direct reports beyond individual goals toward broader organizational achievements (Eagly and Carli 2003; Eagly 2007). This individualized consideration—specifically using a more coaching, mentoring style to understand individual motivations—is "relatively feminine" (Eagly 2007, 5). The transformational leader is viewed as guide, mentor, and coach, and this leadership style allows more solid relationships to form, making for loyal followers (Bass 1995; Eagly 2007; Eagly and Carli 2003). This is not to say that men do not have this ability; great sports coaches (often men) have such traits. John Wooden, the highly revered basketball coach, reinforces the point of leading others to achieve great heights and incredible performance. Eagly explains this coaching style may not be gender specific but rather a more efficient way to achieve results and influence others.

If anything, transformational leadership presents the best of male and female behaviors. It is no surprise that transformational leaders are in demand, given their ability to articulate future goals and develop strategies to reach such goals, using collective, innovative thinking to bring teams and organizations to new heights. Coaching followers is a key component in achieving goals, and such leaders know how to tap into the motivational drivers of each individual on their team. Like yin and yang, this female advantage presents a double-edged sword, particularly in the prevailing mind-set that views women as caregivers and men as authoritative. In some organizations, this authoritative, assertive, competitive style—what Eagly called an "agentic style"—is viewed as efficient and predominantly male. Women are more often viewed as communal and if they exhibit an agentic style chances are they will be judged negatively and fail more frequently (Eagly and Johannesen-Schmidt 2001; Eagly et al. 2003; Eagly 2007).

Imagine the impact on Asian women, often categorized as both communal and self-effacing. The reactions (positive or negative) reflect gender and cultural stereotypes of what leadership looks like and how it practiced. Typically, behavior is processed through a mental blueprint influencing what we see and impacting how we translate it (Fletcher 2002). Transformational qualities—of collaboration and the collective—work well, but not everyone sees the benefits of this style. Projecting into the future, we can see that working in increasingly diverse groups calls for an inclusive style of embracing differences, one that also provides advantages for women and across cultures.

Most leadership research assesses followers, whereas my interest in transformational leaders stems from its connection to women, its application to global organizations, and its focus on the greater good. As Eagly points out, "Good leadership is increasingly defined in terms of the qualities of a good coach or teacher rather of than a highly authoritative person who merely tells others what to do" (Eagly 2007, 3). I used a qualitative method with stories, and did not measure these five traits or interview followers, but rather incorporated the tenets of transformational leadership as both a platform and starting point for my journey. Each of my participants shared stories, openly discussing in a participative and coaching style how this style played out in their work, family relationships, and community.

- Ms. Lee spent considerable time outside of work with young women from her church group, career-coaching them while maintaining a balanced life.
- Ms. Chin returned to school to obtain a coaching certificate. When she leaves the corporate world, she will be an executive coach or work with youth sports teams. "After all, I've been doing this my whole life."

- Ms. Ali, as a professor, focuses on asking challenging questions, mentoring, and coaching young emerging leaders from under-developed countries.
- Ms. Ito shared stories about stepping back to help others achieve success. Running a global nonprofit, she does not see herself as a leader but more as a coach and a guide.

Not only did all interview participants mention the personal benefits gained in the process of coaching others, they frequently referred to themselves in the same manner. When I asked, "Tell me about becoming a leader," the response was, "I'm not a leader, I'm a coach, facilitator, or guide."

Connecting Stories and Research

Researching and facilitating leadership development in organizations, I have read volumes on leadership and worked with many cross-culturally diverse leaders. In the interviews, I listened reflectively, waiting for the story to unfold and to learn from the participants' experiences. As I began writing, I wondered if these women shared common qualities. Integrity was the first quality to surface. Not surprisingly, integrity is part of every competency framework and listed as one of the top two attributes of leaders in Asia (Ray and Learmond 2013). Reading through my notes on each story, I can easily pinpoint a conversation or recall a discussion demonstrating integrity, specifically the women's focus on being authentic and true to their values.

The participants' the stories and experiences were vastly different; the only shared characteristic was gender. Cheung and Halpern (2010), while researching women leaders in Hong Kong, China, and the United States, found more similarities than differences among women across cultures. Reading about the gendered context of leadership, the words "self-determination" and "reflection" surfaced. I could see "determination" demonstrated by all the participants in their overcoming of mental and structural obstacles. Interestingly, organizations spend an inordinate amount of time trying to understand barriers to women's advancement when the solution rests with their constituents. In every story, my participants found ways to overcome cultural, personal, and structural obstacles. These women did not wait for something to change, either through a pivotal event or a different path; they made change happen. In their stories and certainly throughout leadership theory, self-determination, the autonomy to act, and determination to succeed emerge as essential to achievement (Bass 1999).

Constraints also created opportunities. Overcoming barriers fuelled a can-do attitude and fierce determination to succeed in the women I interviewed (Hewlett and Rashid 2011). Strategies for overcoming obstacles and challenges ran the gamut from Ms. Ali's "I'll show you attitude" to Ms. Lee's daily recitation of Shakespeare to learn English. Ms. Chin was catapulted into a leadership position at a young age and realized the value of hard work and the importance of family. Her determination to succeed was further strengthened through competitive sports. The interviews with her are imbued with sporting analogies and reference to team trophies, and it is easy to see the analogy between leadership and team sports. Running a large corporate division, Ms. Chin drew on past experience to bring together a talented team, collectively develop goals, and coach team members through failure and success. As is true with sports, failure calls for reflection, resilience, and asking more from oneself as leader and from the team. These qualities continue to shape her today in her work with her team and family. My participants demonstrated limitless determination to succeed—in their intellectual drive, participation in competitive sports, and their considerable achievements.

Ms. Ito left her home country and family to discover herself. An outsider in a conformist society, she moved away from painful situations and pursued doing good and giving back to the community. Ms. Ito and Ms. Ali are prime examples of leaders who left family behind, challenging tradition, and confronting their culture. They both realized the need to physically separate from family, spending appreciable development and reflective time to become who they are. For both women, authentic behavior and actions are ways of life. Ms. Lee also moved away from family and country for very different reasons. She did not chafe against Chinese culture but migrated to South Africa for university studies and felt at home in this culture. This merging of cultures is beautifully articulated in her comment, "I have an African soul and a Chinese face." Starting her career in South Africa, she began with a strategic plan to move ahead quickly.

Ms. Chin did not believe in too much planning; she confided, "I didn't really plan, but I do believe in very traditional Asian style. If you prove yourself, there are opportunities, and of course you have to go for the opportunity if it's there." Fortuitous events, hard work, and a few great bosses provided opportunities for Ms. Chin's advancement. These women's stories highlight the qualities of transformational leadership and illustrate their determination in the pursuit of achievements for the common good and an understanding of others (Bass 1999).

Authentic, Moral, and Powerful

Authenticity, integrity, and the moral high road were major interview topics. For many women, authenticity is particularly important, operating through values, across multiple boundaries and levels of authority (Kellerman and Rhode 2007). These personal values are motivators but only become transformational when put into action (Ciulla 2004). Ms. Ito could well be emblematic for choosing the high road and putting values into action. The story of Ms. Ito's diseased hands provided powerful insights into herself, and her leadership burned with a renewed sense of purpose. With this pivotal event, she turned the idea of feeding the world into a global giving business. She is acutely aware and driven by what is needed to make the world a better place.

Like Ms. Ito, transformational leaders focus on the bigger issues of social and community concerns, operating beyond concerns of profit, loss, and balanced budgets (Ciulla 2004; Eagly 2007). My participants all embody this spirit; their lives are filled with self-discovery, focused on others, and grounded in ethics. Given the macroenvironment and globalization of work, leadership has moved away from focus on task and reward toward inclusive collaboration to achieve shared goals. Taking a cue from Ms. Ito, contemporary leaders must embody ethics, demonstrate trust, and be adaptable to inspire a diverse community of followers. Women exhibit a leadership style that is not only effective but also fits well into the contemporary, continuously evolving environment (Eagly and Carli 2003).

Except for Ms. Ito, all participants had abundant career choices from medicine, sociology, and economics to business. Ms. Ito had to leave Japan in search of freedom and more favorable choices. Times have changed for women globally, but still far too few women make it to the top, despite having the "right stuff" for leadership. The working world has changed but organizational systems lag woefully behind. To close the gap, a few organizations using targets or quotas, when instead they should focus on embracing differences, being inclusive, and changing mind-sets. Targets are short-term stratagems, whereas changing an attitude or behavior to allow for differences is a long-term strategy.

Organizations have evolved beyond hierarchies toward flatter structures and partnerships. This shift places greater emphasis on using the "soft power" of influence, collaboration, and inclusive behavior. "Soft power," a term coined by Joseph Nye, the former dean of the Kennedy School of Government at Harvard, has definite links to global leadership and multinational organizations. Nye views soft power as the ability to persuade and shape opinions without strong-arm tactics to resolve conflict and achieve results. Soft power conjures up images of Mahatma Gandhi, and today is represented by Lena Ben Mehnini, Asma Mahfouz, and Mona Eltahawey, all Arab Spring activists who are the new face of soft power and use a collective voice to promote equality through democracy.

Burns (2010) did not use the term soft power but describes transformational leaders in similar words. Moving away from coercive power, transformational leaders understand power through relationships, relying on collaboration and persuasion in order to reach shared goals. Working through partnerships and using "so-called feminine values" (Eisler 2005, 22) of coaching, indirect communication, and soft power resonates across collective cultures throughout Asia Pacific (Eisler 2005; Trompenaars 1997; Earley et al. 2006; Bergsten et al. 2008). Transformational, morally centered leadership is not merely a feminine style but a strong leadership style connected with globally diverse communities.

Building an Inclusive, Integrated Web

Leadership is no longer exclusively authoritative, but centered and connected. Sally Helgesen discovered this centered style through narrative research with four women executives in the United States.

Her book *The Female Advantage: Women's Ways of Leadership,* published in the late 1990s, became an international bestseller. Helgesen believed organizations needed a new way of organizing, leading, and engaging talent. While completing my master's degree in organizational design, I read *The Female Advantage,* revisited her work, and corresponded with Helgesen during this project. In her book, Helgesen shared a story about Frances Hesselbein, the former chief executive officer of the Girl Scouts. Over dinner at the Cosmopolitan Club where paper and pen were not allowed, Frances illustrated her organizational structure and demonstrated how she led, using the condiments on the table: a pepper mill, cups, saucers, and eating utensils. Hesselbein placed a pepper mill in the middle of the dining table. "This is me, in the center of the organization" (Helgesen 1995, 45) and Helgesen's "web of inclusion" (41) was born.

In describing the web, Hesselbein explained centered leadership by placing herself in the middle of a circular organizational chart, as these circles were symbolically important to her (1995). The leader is "the heart rather than the head, and so does not need layers and ranks below to reinforce status" (1995, 55). The web works through connections and relationships rather than through power over or distance from the team. This style of leading is aligned with "partner-oriented societies" (Eisler 2005, 21), with flattened organizational structures, and with use of soft power to achieve results. Realizing the broader implications of the web, Helgesen has since moved this idea from the individual to the field of organizational design.

More recently, researchers for *McKinsey Quarterly* (Barsh et al. 2008) examined this approach to women's leadership with a similar centered, whole-self concept. Interviewing women and men globally, the researchers found five interconnected leadership dimensions: (1) finding meaning, strengths, and purpose; (2) using energy and knowing how to draw upon this force; (3) framing the world from a positive perspective; (4) building connections and valuing relationships for business and personal growth; and (5) engaging, finding voice, confidence, accepting opportunities and risks (Barsh et al. 2008).

These dimensions connect to Helgensen's web of inclusion, Cheung and Halpern's research, and my participants' stories. I found a pattern of inclusiveness, specifically that of building a uniquely

Asian web. Helgesen mentions family as part of this web, and I too found family, particularly the Asian definition of extended family, an integral part of the path to success. Interviewing Ms. Chin, I found she had a story similar to Hesselbein's on leading from the center, physically placing herself in the middle of an open office (and on the organizational chart) surrounded by a talented team of managers. She emphasized on numerous occasions the importance of hiring talented managers, "ones that were smarter than me." For Ms. Chin the web extends and expands beyond work. Within the web she also placed her family, including her mother, husband, children, aunts, uncles, nieces, nephews, nannies, and drivers. Ms. Chin admitted, "I am the pampered one. I have two helpers who have been with me for over 10 years." The next rung on the web combined her sports community with family and work colleagues. The final rung comprised her social community and board activities. This expansive web is inclusive and interconnected, pulling diverse constituents into the center. Like Hesselbein, she does not feel constricted, controlled, or boxed in (Helgesen 1995) and does not see the need to separate work and life. Her success comes from integrating work, personal or family life, and community.

Similarly, Cheung and Halpern's (2010) interviews with 62 executive women in Hong Kong, China, and the United States found related patterns of merging families with work. As was true with my participants, "each lived one life rather than two separate lives at work and at home, they created links between family and work, although they kept their role identities distinct" (2010, 185). The ongoing organizational discussions on work and life balance were out of sync with the way Asian women were leading; rather, a connected, integrated way of working offered them harmony, stability, and efficiency (Cheung and Halpern 2010).

Based on all these stories, family support is critical. Sheryl Sandberg's popular book *Lean In: Women, Work, and the Will to Lead* (2013) highlights the importance of having an equal partner. Cheung and Halpern (2010) support Sandberg's statement on finding an equal partner. In my research, the partner is important, but in Asia the support of extended family plays a pivotal role. Ms. Chin told me, "Without my husband and family support, I would not be here today." Ms. Lee's web of inclusion determines not only how she leads, but it is also her lifeline for success. She reinforced this, stating,

"Without my family and church group, I would not be successful." The stories of Ms. Chin and Ms. Lee mirror Frances Hesselbein's story, and for each of these women family is the central component. Early on, Ms. Ali remained physically separated from her family, but she has since reunited with them. Through her marriage (to a non-Bangladeshi) she relocated to Bangladesh and remains close to her family. Ms. Ito's work community has become her extended family. In contrast to the Western definition of family, three of my participants thought of family as representing a wide range of distant and close relatives (along with hired help, who can easily also be viewed as family). Reflecting on Ms. Hesselbein's web shows that the focus remained on her immediate family. My participants defined community even more broadly to include team, church, sports, and other groups. Ms. Chin and Ms. Lee did not discuss work and family separately and seldom referred to either work or family competing for time. This elastic web of inclusion stretches across multiple communities, linking work and family, and as discussed by Cheung and Halpern, it provided efficiencies and stability.

The definition of family highlights subtle cultural differences. In addition, the web emphasizes harmony within these diverse communities. If any element is out of sync, the entire web is impacted. The focus on harmony reflects the collectivistic values representative of my participants' cultural backgrounds. This integration of work and family in Japan, Bangladesh, Taiwan, and Singapore dates back centuries to family-run enterprises. In China, this interconnected web represents a network of relationships providing stability during uncertain periods (Bond 1991). For my participants, this philosophy enabled successful leadership transitions when they could rely on this interconnected web while managing career transitions. In contrast, Western societies favor independence and the self, whereas collectivist societies place significance on interdependence and group orientation (Cheung and Halpern 2010; Trompenaars 1997; Earley et al. 2006; Swenson 2009). In Bangladesh, this collective style is one of the fundamentals of Islamic leadership (Swenson 2009; Hussain and Mohideen 2010).

McKinsey's centered leadership defines the dimension on connecting as, "identifying who can help you grow, building stronger relationships and increasing your sense of belonging" (Barsh 2008, 36). My participant's stories underscored the importance of developing an inclusive and people-centric web. As with McKinsey, the focus is on relationships, but the emphasis is guiding and coaching, allowing solid relationships to form while developing loyal followers. My participants ascended the ranks of leadership, and so did their followers, all sharing a "lift as you climb" mentality and a very real sense of giving back to their community. Ms. Chin and Ms. Lee repeatedly mentioned coaching others to success and pursuing shared goals and creating an inclusive work place. Ms. Ito's and Ms. Ali's sole purpose is giving back to their communities; for Ms. Ito this community extends to the entire globe.

Reflection, Mindfulness, and Spirituality

Throughout my research, finding purpose became a central theme. McKinsey's centered leadership refers to "meaning or finding your strengths and putting them in the service of an inspiring purpose" (Barsh et al. 2008, 36). The four women I interviewed shared stories of reflection and serendipitous moments of realization to uncover purpose and find renewal. Reflection appeared in many forms, from mindfulness with Ms. Ito, prayers with Ms. Lee, and spirituality with Ms. Ali. While Ms. Chin discussed personal reflections, the others spoke candidly about spirituality and religiosity. These reflective periods in various formats provided an avenue for quiet confrontation with culture, tradition, and beliefs.

During our interviews, Ms. Lee used spirituality and religion interchangeably. She referred to her work as a "calling," attributed it to a religious sect and linked it to a belief in a higher power or united with purpose and passion (Krishnakumar and Neck 2002). Practicing her religion and being part of a religious community is how she leads her team and sees life. She viewed her faith as allowing her to drive transformational change in organizations. Her stories of leadership and personal vision are embedded within the same beliefs and were used to engage her team. This spiritual belief not only transforms organizations but also brings reflection and self-discovery into the workforce (Dent et al. 2005). Ms. Ali, on the other hand, firmly articulated spirituality not linked to any religion. Her adamant words and strong opinion stem from personal struggles with organized religion, specifically Islam. Ms. Ito discussed spirituality in terms of self and of being mindful and present. With Ms. Ito, genuine renewal required mindfulness and a reflective turn inward to make sense of the world. Her nomadic journey from Japan through North America, Europe, and Asia included periods of renewal and rejuvenation mixed with deep emotion and pain. For Ms. Ito and Ms. Ali, spirituality became the essence of life, an acute awareness shaping how they showed up at work and for our interviews (Howard 2002; Krishnakumar and Neck 2002; Korac-Kakabadse et al. 2002; Avolio and Gardner 2005); Ms. Chin, a Buddhist, did not dwell deeply on the topic but instead referred to hard work, sports, and shared stories of reflection.

Spirituality, like leadership, is often loosely defined despite many attempts to clarify the concept (Dent et al. 2005). In organizations, the topic surfaces and submerges, depending on overall conditions. The retirement of baby boomers and chaos in global markets coincides with an increase in discussions of spirituality (Dent et al. 2005). Spirituality, for some, is an integral part of organizational life, whereas others "avoid the topic given the negative connotations of proselyte, the evangelical right, or undue influence of subordinate behavior" (Tischler et al. 2002, 210). For employees (as for my participants), spirituality brings calm to an otherwise chaotic and stressful, pressurized world (Lips-Wiersma and Mills 2002). The changing nature of work and blurring of boundaries opens the door for spirituality to enter organizations, and the workplace sometimes becomes a surrogate family. My participants fused work and life, with community and team becoming part of their extended family.

Research indicates that women spend time exploring spirituality and purpose as a dimension of leadership (Coughlin et al. 2005; Buck 2007). This deep introspective period often begins at midlife or in midcareer, leading to a questioning of purpose and search for meaning in life (Vickers-Willis 2002). Other than midlife, a pivotal work or life event can generate similar reflections. Quantitative research indicates there is "no relationship between transformational leadership and spirituality" (Tischler et al. 2002, 209), but qualitative research suggests otherwise, showing a connection between ethics, authenticity, honesty, and integrity (Dent et al. 2005; Krishnakumar and Neck 2002; Avolio and Gardner 2005). Given the ambiguous definitions of leadership and spirituality, the quantitative results

are puzzling. Reflection and self-awareness in leadership development lend support to the connection to spirituality. Many contemporary leadership theories have links to Christianity, Mormonism,
Taoism, Confucianism, Hinduism, Islam, and other organized religions (Krishnakumar and Neck 2002; Korac-Kakabadse et al. 2002;
Mattson 2005).

Nancy Adler's work in researching global leadership led her to
believe leadership must have a spiritual component (1997). Like
Adler, I found many references to discussions of spiritually, religion,
and leadership with my participants. Spirituality for Ms. Ito and
Ms. Ali originates from a moral purpose, whereas Ms. Lee retained
ties to her religious affiliation. For Ms. Ali, leadership is grounded
in morals, authenticity, and relationship with others. Listening to
their stories, I found it difficult to separate spirituality and religious
beliefs from leadership. This makes sense, as leaders do not leave
their beliefs at the reception door—like everyone else, they bring
their whole self to work.

The Path Forward

Addressing the United Nations, Hillary Clinton stated, "Empowering
women means a more stable world economy" (Richman 2011).
Clinton's comments reverberated globally, but especially so in
Asia, with a major economic focus to encourage women to remain
in the workforce. In Bangladesh, seeing the connection between
education and economic growth, the government plans to allevi-
ate poverty through empowerment and education of girls. Prime
Minister Sheikh Hasina has been both praised and vilified for her
role in the advancement of women and eradication of poverty. She
is praised by the UN for empowering women and criticized for
her government's interventions with Grameen Bank, where women
are the main beneficiaries of the bank (Krystoff 2012). In Japan,
Prime Minister Abe has called for targets to increase the number of
women in senior positions in all industries. He too has received a
mixed response. Abe's reform calls for more childcare facilities and
training for women returning to work. Yet he and others hold on
to the belief that women should have primary care responsibilities.
The underrepresentation of women will not be alleviated by day

care. Deep cultural traditions and attitudes remain. Kathy Matsui at Goldman Sachs states if women participation increases from 60 percent to 80 percent, the gross domestic product will increase by 14 percent (Torres 2013; Matsui et al. 2010). Japan needs women to rebuild the economy but most remain locked in a cultural strait-jacket. In Malaysia, Prime Minister Najib pushes for equal represen-tation with a goal of having 55 percent of women in the workforce, and he links this contribution to achieving developed nation status. All of these are powerful economic drivers of change.

Countries in Asia must now calculate the high cost of struc-tural barriers and outdated traditions of women remaining in low-paying positions, earning significantly less yet living appreciably longer than men. These barriers range from mandatory retirement age, disruption of family communities, lack of child care, and long-held beliefs on the role of women. Day care and flexible schedules are beneficial, but collectively confronting deeply rooted mind-sets will have more lasting impact. This starts with taking a critical look at leadership selection and having the courage to challenge atti-tudes. Finding a way to overcome barriers makes growth possible and achieves economic goals for Asia and the rest of the world.

Over the past decade and for the foreseeable future, emerging leaders will need to engender trust, model morality, and demon-strate adaptability. Organizations must be open to embrace dif-ferences. Leadership models must quickly and accurately reflect changing demographics and cultural differences. While women have made significant advances in the workforce, there is still con-fusion around traditional feminine qualities and notions associ-ated with leadership (Dawley et al. 2004; Eagly and Carli 2003). Current leadership models highlight the pernicious and persistent problems for women and multicultural groups. Although demo-graphics drive change, organizations need to acknowledge and act on these differences, moving forward with a new definition of leadership. This definition must take into account the benefits of soft power, the value of family, and importance of bringing the whole self to work. Organizations must move past the one-size-fits-all model and accept that effective leadership can be exercised by both men and women.

This chapter has explored the many different prisms of leader-ship: transformational leadership, McKinsey's centered leadership,

Helgesen's web of inclusion, and Cheung and Halpern's cross-cultural perspective. Looking to the future, what type of leaders do we need for organizations? Certainly moral ones with the ability to build trust, connect with diverse groups, and navigate multicultural complexities. To do so, leadership selection requires courage and open-mindedness on both sides of the boardroom to build gender-balanced, globally inclusive work environments that focus on the greater good.

What Are the Next Steps?

The progressive steps are to build a new view of leadership and improve the selection process. The essence of leadership is building relationships and coalitions for good. These relationships are multifaceted, interconnected, real, virtual, long-term, short-term, intimate, formal, pithy, or loquacious. But the foundation of any good leadership is in values. Putting these elements into the mix, leadership must be highly inclusive. Recent research by the Conference Board (Ray and Learmond 2013) indicates this shift is in progress, with organizations expanding the definition of leadership, basing it on values, rather than personality traits, simplifying leadership models, and embracing a global perspective. This change will only be achieved when organizations mirror the diversity of the marketplace—across all levels.

One of the biggest issues facing organizations today is retaining talent, developing emerging leaders, and ensuring leadership for the future. In Asia, this issue is complicated by extreme conditions: economic growth combined with abject poverty, advanced education and mass illiteracy, extreme longevity and declining populations. The only constant is change. While statistics paint a bleak picture of the talent gap, there is talent in the market, but it is often overlooked when people use an opaque lens.

Sheryl Sandberg raised awareness on the role of women in the workforce. It is time for organizations to take the next step. Previous programs, using targets and development programs exclusively for women, have fallen short of their well-meant goals. A target does not build inclusivity but rather deepens the divide. What is required is better problem solving and different interventions to ensure success.

The problem is not a dearth of women. The challenge is navigating a monocultural maze. The solution is not found in making one side conform. The resolution rests with valuing the attributes of both men and women. Certainly there are challenges on both sides of the equation with some women retreating from opportunities and some organizations overlooking talented women.

Transformational leadership is androgynous, combining the best of both male and female behavior. The full range of leadership is needed: authentic, inclusive, and spiritual.
Organizations should

1. move away from outworn competency frameworks and examine leadership based on values;
2. take educated risks on people and provide support to navigate transitions;
3. scrutinize structural barriers and question sacred cows in compensation practices and leadership selection;
4. put on an Asian lens to understand the rhythms of life;
5. tap into this inclusive web, appreciate how inclusion sustains success, drives innovation, and builds organizational efficiency; and
6. nurture the collective voices to value differences.

CHAPTER 9

Multicultural Mishaps

> Riding the crest of globalization and technology, English dominates the world as no language ever has.
>
> Seth Mydans 2007

A recent post in one of the LinkedIn groups on diversity and Inclusion stated, "Fortunately, we're all different." Of course we are; yet, it appears that many organizations continue to seek a staid conformity around a set of leadership models. The Internet is entwined with globalization, increasingly defusing many sharp differences, blending (or "blanding") cultures, obscuring identities, and sanding over leadership definitions.

If leadership becomes difficult to define, it then follows that otherwise easy profiles get convoluted—so much so that "multiculturalism," "becoming multicultural" and "understanding cultures" (terms used throughout this book) may slide into obsolescence. JoAnn Phillion's (2002) research on multicultural narrative was the fillip for using narrative inquiry. I was captivated by Phillion's research on multicultural education; her paper read like a novel of magical realism. She captured elliptical stories, filled with dance scenes and dreams, providing an evocative tale of Canadian multicultural schools. In her research, the main character, Ms. Multicultural, embodies interpretive characteristics and distills truths of cross-cultural inquiry. Phillion's themes foreshadow this chapter's issues: confusion about cultural identity, confrontation with words, and challenges with outdated frameworks and applying this learning to organizational life and leadership selection.

Cultural Identity

We carry our cultural baggage with us; we are filled with values, emotions, and truths we hold close. To work and research in diverse environments must begin with an exploration of these truths to better understand ourselves and our perspectives. The study of culture is a fascinating subject, conjuring up the names of Margaret Mead, Ruth Benedict, Franz Boas, and others. In the late 1980s, cultural anthropology hit a crisis with the publication of *Writing Culture: The Poetics and Politics of Ethnography*, edited by James Clifford and George Marcus. On one hand, the book garnered accolades for the analysis and bringing greater awareness to the discipline. On the other hand, only one woman contributed to the book, which caused a flurry among women writers and many cultural anthropologists. When asked why, Clifford's response was, "women anthropologists were excluded because their writings failed to fit the requirements of being feminist *and* textually innovative" (1995, 5). Incensed by such an exclusion, Ruth Behar and Deborah Gordon delivered a collection of creative and critical essays, combining history, culture, and a feminist response, *Women Writing Culture* (1995). Their book provides different perspectives on anthropology and clearly places women at the center. Clifford's comments were not viewed as malicious but thought to be more "masculine subjectivity" (1995, 5). One would think such bantering is out of vogue today. However, the lack of diversity in both boardrooms and executive suites consistently influence leadership selection.

I embarked on this research seeing myself as Ms. Multicultural, embodying cultural elements and interpretations of multicultural research. While Phillion carried "distilled truths" into her research (2002, 267), I carried my own bag of diverse values and mental models. Working in Asia provided me with a different prism for understanding leadership. Holding both American and Irish passports and with permanent residency in Hong Kong, I thought this difference would be detectable. I had left the United States in the late 1980s to move to Changsha, China, teaching English to graduate student engineers. Before moving to China, all teachers were required to participate in two-week intensive cross-cultural training and a three-month immersion course in Chinese language. At the end of these sessions, I knew more about the language than I did about the culture. (That's not saying much, as I remain a linguistic novice of Mandarin). While this move changed my view of the world, my values and sense of self were already formed (Gardner 2010). This is an important distinction, impacting personal perspectives and world views. Like my participants, I left my home country but carried my (American) values with me. Values, formed at an early age, remain dormant or embedded within our psyche until we're confronted to apply them, and this makes it difficult (although not impossible) to change perspectives, shift thinking, or accept different views.

Between globalization and technology and attempting to understand cultures, cultural identity becomes a tangled web. When I gave a talk to graduate recruits at a Swiss bank, I saw clues to the challenges for global organizations. A typical profile of these participants would be: twenty-something Asian, American, or European, primary school in Asia, secondary boarding school in the United Kingdom, university and graduate school at an Ivy League school, language immersion in Spain, France, or China. It is difficult to place this group of graduates into one culture or one category. Although older, my participants mirrored the same profile.

I started my interviews with what I thought was a "soft" question: "Where is home?" Pollock and Van Reken (1999) started with the same question in their book, *The Third Culture Kid Experience*. A third-culture kid is described as a "generic term to discuss the lifestyle created, shared, and learned by those who are from one culture and are in the process of relating to another one" (1999, 21). My participants could be categorized as global nomads or third-culture adults, but each tag carries a different meaning and connotation (Horan 2012). This definition was not exactly the right fit, as my participants were confused by a question of identity or home, having lived most of their time away from their home country.

Listening to my participants' responses and reflecting on my presentation to young bankers, I became intrigued with cultural hybrids, multiculturalism, and citizenship mutations (Ong 1995; Probyn 1996; Phillion 2002). As I read more on this topic, I moved from cultural hybrid to cultural identity. This subject provides an eclectic mix of insights and a loose framework for how to consider future leaders. Identity is discussed from an eclectic perspective: birth certificates, professions, religious affiliation, education, and a host of other criteria (Maalouf 2011). Certainly this is an improvement over erroneously linking home or identity to passports. It is frankly hard to believe that a passport, a small book with a regulation-size photo and a couple of lines on birth origin could represent identity (Sarup and Raja 1996; Appiah 2006). How many passports did my participants have? Ms. Chin, a citizen of Singapore, had only one. Even with this passport, she proudly stated, "I am Chinese." In contrast, Singapore's founding father, Lee Kwan Yuen, is quoted as saying, "I am no more Chinese than John Kennedy was an Irishman" (Buruma 1996, 283). Assuredly, passports, heritage, and identity are difficult to declare or pinpoint.

Montouri (2013) writes about the "global mutt" (2013, 5), mutt being a term borrowed from President Obama, and rebranded as global. Global mutts live significantly long periods outside their country of passport before becoming citizens of another country, usually but not always the host country. This description fits Ms. Ito, but not the other participants. Ford (2011) uses the phrase "rubber-band nationality" (2011, 5), an elastic concept borrowed from Carolyn Smith's work with third-culture kids. However, this concept has broader applications. Three of my participants have dual citizenship, speak several languages, and spent significant time outside their home country. Ms. Ito, Japanese, lived in North America, Central America, and Asia Pacific, and she speaks English, Spanish, and Japanese. When I interviewed Ms. Ito, it was difficult to separate Japanese values from the other cultural influences. Reflecting on her story of firing herself publicly, this ritualistic act of honor demonstrated deep Japanese values of saving face and showing respect. Ms. Ali refers to herself as a citizen of the world and is perhaps more representative of a "rubber-band nationality"

(Ford 2011, 155); she has moved effortlessly through many cultures. She was born in Bangladesh, spent formative years in Thailand, and then moved to Canada for university and graduate school. Fluent in several languages, moving between multiple interpretations of Islam, Ms. Ali is difficult to categorize. Ms. Lee is Taiwanese but claims to be African in her soul. Although Chinese, she did not feel "at home" in the People's Republic of China. I can see the applicability of Montouri's global mutt, but calling Ms. Lee by that moniker doesn't ring right.

While these women's frames of reference are different, I see similarities and differences to my life. Ms. Lee's statement of having an African soul is very powerful. Based on my nearly thirty years of experience, I may see myself as Asian but look Caucasian. If I start a conversation in Mandarin few will listen and most will answer in English. I cannot rid myself of being "the American." Interestingly enough, Ford highlights that many American women living in Hong Kong make an "ongoing effort to mask their 'Americanness'" (2011, 6). Ms. Lee may feel African in body, voice, and soul but may also face the same challenges. These assumptions about both of us are based on visual appearance and voice. My whiteness/Americanness is defined in voice, language, and physical features. No matter how long I live here, I will always be a white American. The same views confront women in the workforce. It does not make any difference how many women enter the workforce as long as assumptions about careers, leadership, and commitment remain unchanged. When I facilitate workshops on unconscious bias with a diverse community of professionals, someone almost always asks, "Do women really want to work in [...name any industry]?" The room, half filled with women, provides the answer. Old habits and thinking remain about culture and gender roles.

Word Confusion

Doing research across diverse cultures can be disorienting and bewildering at times. On many occasions I found myself tangled up in a web of words, attempting to make sense of the meaning. As much as I thought I knew about multicultural work environments, I stumbled over the basic element of language. English maybe the global language of business, but words across cultures are interpreted differently. Words tug on our values. Language—in particular the emotional content carried by words—can have a formidable impact on multicultural research. Meanings remain fragmented unless researchers (similar to organizations) dig beneath the surface. Three words proved challenging and nearly hindered my progress: "ambition," "failure," and "leader." These same words are heard every day at work.

Words flowed easily to formulate my research questions but failed miserably during my interviews. Robert Frost said, "Words exist in the mouth not in books. You can't fix them, and you don't want to fix them. You want them to adapt their sounds to persons and places and times. You want them to change and be different" (Barry 1973, 45). This may be true for poets but not for me. The words existed in my mind but not in my participants' response. I wanted their answers to be different. Unlike Frost, I wanted to fix the words. Instead, language rocked my foundation, leaving me grappling with the material to create a story.

A basic element and a major force in language is the written word. The French Algerian philosopher Jacques Derrida believed that in reading we fill gaps to create meaning (Agger 1991). Derrida has written extensively on language and meaning, specifically the arbitrariness and difficulty translating expressions across cultures. Following this thinking, we need to accept that language is impure, to understand the context requires time to read, review, and reflect. Only then will the gaps be filled. While conducting this research, I had the time to review my interview notes and reread my stories. Yet, this luxury of time may not be the case inside organizations. At work, we may not have the time to listen, and we rarely have the time to read someone's story. We may hear a "30 second" elevator pitch or read a short blurb when a new leader joins, but words on paper are flat devoid of context. Most corporate announcements are formulaic, leaving little room for personal anecdotes or stories.

It is indeed fortunate that we're all different, all seeing the world from a unique perspective. To appreciate these differences, we need to peel back layers to examine context and uncover meaning. Words challenged my beliefs. I thought I had a strong understanding of cultural subtleties, but words eluded me, exposing me to different interpretations and diverse perspectives.

Pulling together a cross-cultural narrative on leadership and telling the story of four distinctly different women began with self-doubt as I was unsure whether I could find my way. The first challenge came when I asked my participants to describe a time when they had failed. The response was silence or "I have not failed" or "life has always been good to me." I wrote in the side column of my notes, "Truth? Or culturally correct?" For many of us, life is upheaval, chaos, bliss. Howard Gardner's book *Leading Minds: An Anatomy of Leadership* (1995) shaped my questions. Gardner studied historical figures in business, government, and academia and found six constant features of leadership, one of which was overcoming setbacks through resilience. Failure in Silicon Valley, for example, is a badge of honor. Failing multiple times is even better, increasing status and value. In China and Japan, failure links with losing face and does not carry the same medal of adoration. Leadership programs use this same framework to simulate setbacks to see how participants bounce back. I was far from content with the responses I received, so I did what most interviewers do: I asked the question again from a different angle. However, I received the same answers. In each case I continued with the interview despite the flat, emotionless responses.

But I had overlooked the significance of the word "failure." I used an American leadership feature when asking questions of a diverse community of women. In hindsight, I was narrowly focused on finishing the story and not allowing time to learn from their experiences. The goal of completing the story nearly derailed the objective of this study, specifically that of understanding leadership from my participants' experience. This same achievement-oriented focus is rewarded in organizations. Most if not all competency frameworks have *driving for results* as a key component of leadership. To me, this is a given; most of us enter organizations wanting to achieve results. Reflecting on my experience in this study and at work, I realized that *driving for results* also applies in the selection process. Managers often complain about not having enough time to recruit talent. Either because of constraints of supply and demand or mounting pressure from business, the process is frequently rushed. Rushing these decisions does not guarantee that the best candidate is chosen and does not remove blind spots in the selection process.

In my research, did I hear or interpret answers correctly? Similar misinterpretations occur during talent or leadership selection with women. DDI, a human resource think tank, found that more women than men fall off the talent ladder (Howard and Wellins 2008/2009) and were left out of leadership development programs. The researchers assumed this lack of access to developmental programs hindered the women's opportunities for advancement. But a single program doth not make a leader. The bigger question is: Why do women fall off the ladder in the first place? Women fall out of talent plans because they do not fit the prevailing leadership model that emphasizes being visible, vocal, and commanding presence. Yet presence is an ambiguous term; the definition is connected to context, culture, and feeling. To have more women enrolled in talent plans, organizations need to reexamine their selection criteria, define ambiguous concepts, review their competency definitions, and look at their decision-making process.

In addition to talent selection, performance reviews provide other challenges. They are a prime example of organizationally misdirected words and abuse of power. The problem stems from the subjective nature of the process, communication style differences, and misinterpretations of words. Sam Culbert and Lawrence Rout in their book *Get Rid of Performance Reviews* (2010) discuss the philosophy underlying the review process and the challenges with objectivity. Instead of reviewing past job performance, they suggest managers should project forward, previewing a collaborative and iterative process to effectively plan and achieve goals. I would also add that this process maintains face. Conducting a "preview" leans toward the positive with (I assume) more feedback. Cross-culturally and with a multigenerational workforce previews are more productive. Well-intended performance reviews often fall short of the stated goals. A recent lawsuit against a highly regarded multinational organization highlights the challenges regarding language and performance reviews. The lawsuit was initiated by a group of successful women executives who found they were being replaced by younger, men. The organization had used the performance review process to demote or terminate and offer severance packages to the women. The reviews measured qualities such as "having a killer instinct, being aggressive and assertive, being succinct, and making quick decisions, cutting to the quick with information, commanding attention, and having leadership skills" (Carter 2010). Similarly, Cheung and Halpern (2010) found references in recruitment documents to aggressive closers, compelling communicators, and independent leaders. These qualities underscored issues with words and a subjective, biased evaluation process. Cheung and Halpern (2010) suggest expanding the definition of leadership to include exerting influence, a skill women have always had in greater amounts than men. Quantitative research contradicts this statement; however, there are style differences, which are not necessarily gender-specific but situation-relevant. Women, more than men, use a consultative, inspirational, or engaging approach (Merchant 2012). Merchant's research on influencing styles connects with Eagly's notion of idealized influence or using a coaching style to engage others. Given this connection to selling styles, it is hard to believe that "having influence or the ability to influence" is not on the above-quoted list of features in the performance reviews.

Word Failure

Along with dictionary definitions, we need greater appreciation for language nuances and a "feeling for words" (Speedy 2008, 67). The word "failure" exposed deeply rooted Confucian values. A guiding Confucian axiom is to stand strong and "contemplate errors behind closed doors" (Debarry et al. 2011, 566). Even 2500 years after Confucius, these traditions remain alive in Japan, Korea, Singapore, Vietnam, Hong Kong, Taiwan, and China (Fu et al. 2008; Ko et al. 2003). What underlies culture are values, some of which are universal—integrity, for example, would be considered ubiquitous. Others are local—saving face would fall into this category (Appiah 2006). This Confucian value, prevailing for thousands of years, reveals that failure is rarely discussed in public.

Going back to the origin of the word in Confucian cultures, failure is connected to the Chinese word, "*lian,*" associated with moral integrity (Trompenaars 1997; Fairbank 1992). The concept of saving face is difficult to articulate and understand in English. Both Chinese and Japanese languages have many words depicting face, shame, and the attached emotions. As in North American culture, "shame" elicits a similar response and is rarely discussed. Shame conjures up disgrace and connotes loss of power and control (Brown 2004). The word "shame" refers to individual control, but "face" concerns the entire lineage: family, extended family, and ancestral heritage. The tradition of honoring ancestors continues today with *Qingming Jie,* or tomb sweeping ceremonies. For example, when my Chinese colleague selected the University of California over Stanford, her mother admonished, "What will your ancestors think?"

Language patterns and structure may reveal subtleties of differences, but deeper insight comes from understanding the emotional impact of words. Language, like art, requires taking a step back or moving closer to understand the context from different angles (Foucault 1994). A culture of 24/7 work leaves little time to understand the context of communication. Conducting research and writing these stories, I had the luxury of time to evaluate and reflect. At work, taking time to reflect is a luxury and not necessarily supported. While facilitating leadership seminars with a group of executive women in India, I asked similar questions and received very different responses. These groups shared colorful stories of hardship and struggles akin to Bollywood movies. These stories were dramatically different from the reactions in Singapore, Taiwan, Japan, and Bangladesh, as failure was not discussed openly, certainly not with outsiders.

Language content is obscured by context. Sixty years ago, Edward T. Hall, anthropologist and cross-cultural researcher, examined communication style differences among indigenous populations in America and across cultures. Hall placed cultures on a continuum of high and low context. He found low-context cultures prefer direct communication, using succinct language and literal interpretation of words. In contrast, indirect communicators often situated in high-context cultures relied more on nonverbal cues.

In my research, literal translations did not work and had the potential to derail this project. Organizations grapple with the same issues. Stylistic differences cut across gender and organizational functions (Tannen 1994). Organizations in the United States take pride in developing global leaders, but they are often rigidly training everyone to communicate in a similar pattern or style. Women's leadership development is now headed down the same path with a specific focus on communication skills. Given the global workforce organizations should reconsider training programs reinforcing or mirroring the prevailing mindset and begin to see and value differences.

There is no denying that language structure, speech patterns, and nonverbal communication all add complexity to cross-cultural inquiry. The same is true in leadership selection. If words I choose present obstacles for my participants, imagine the challenges facing organizations. Words organizations use to select leaders are stuck in competency frameworks, which have existed since the 1960s but with little adaptation (Bolden and Gosling 2006). Originating in the United States and the United Kingdom, these frameworks and subsequent interpretations inadvertently created barriers for women and cultures. For contemporary organizations, language differences present one hurdle; defining leadership raises the bar even higher. There is much to consider and more to juggle with diverse work environments. As organizations become aware of communication challenges and outmoded competencies, judging someone's potential using these "distilled truths" (Phillion 2002, 267) no longer makes sense.

Questions about Words

After analyzing the word "failure," what can we now conclude about the word "leader"? As discussed previously, the language of leadership emanates from Western culture, and the term "leader" did not resonate with any of my participants. This was not a question of misunderstanding the definition. They did not call themselves leaders. Ms. Ali and Ms. Ito referred to themselves as teachers, coaches, guides, or facilitators. Ms. Lee and Ms. Chin viewed themselves as coaches. These coaching values described by my participants connect with transformational leadership qualities, but this label (considering the meaning of the word) might sound too grand to be used comfortably. The humble quality of these women came through vividly, a self-effacing attribute more obvious than their reluctance to discuss failure. Research conducted with midcareer university students in the United States had similar responses (Montouri 2010). This is a gender issue, a global issue, and a generational one and it reflects how leadership is changing.

My misguided reactions to my participants' responses gave me greater appreciation of linguistic cultural nuances. In Vietnam, "leader" and "ambition" triggered different emotional responses.

When I taught an Executive MBA program in Vietnam, one participant found it difficult to answer questions about being a leader. In her opinion, a leader in Vietnam is typically older and often linked with government. Facilitating a discussion on good and bad leaders, the MBA students found ambition to be a negative quality. Reading through their lists, I suggested moving the word "ambitious" into the list of characteristics of a good leader. The room exploded with a resounding, "No!" The program took place in Ho Chi Minh City, and I learned a language lesson. In Vietnamese the word "ambitious" or *"tham vong"* brings together "greed and expectations or unrealistic hope," which carries a negative feeling—and is not something many Vietnamese would want as a label. When I interviewed successful women in Korea, "ambitious" elicited the same reactions. I've had similar responses across multiple cultures in Asia. In Singapore, when working with a group of midcareer women executives I asked the same question. The group preferred the word, "contribution" to ambition. Interestingly enough, organizations can measure a contribution but may not be able to evaluate the impact of ambition. Cheung and Halpern (2010) did not find any references to ambition when they were researching women executives. This is not only an Asian aversion to this word, Marie Wilson's (2007) book, *Closing the Leadership Gap: Add Women, Change Everything*, states, "Ambition in men is an expectation and a virtue. In women, it can be the kiss of death."(2007, 55).

Sheryl Sandberg has different thoughts on ambition and women. She encourages women to be more vocal and intentional about careers and ambitions. Her book, *Lean In*, has become a feminist manifesto for the twenty-first century, raising readers' consciousness about women as equal partners and formidable leaders in the workforce. Sandberg should be commended for increasing awareness, but some of her messages will not easily work across Asia.

For example, a consulting firm based in Hong Kong sought my advice to work with a group of emerging leaders. The firm wanted to ensure equal representation of women, specifically Asian women on track for partnership. Working with several members of this top team, I found all had the academic pedigree for success—an Ivy League education coupled with multilingual skills and a successful track record of client engagements. One consultant in particular stood out, Ms. Lin. Ms. Lin, Malaysian Chinese,

Cambridge graduate, fluent in Mandarin, Cantonese, Malay, and English, small in stature, and highly intelligent was viewed by her clients as a trusted advisor. Ms. Lin's only flaw, according to the partner panel, was that she was perhaps too "ambitious" with an overtly direct communication style that was perceived as brusque within the firm.

A skilled problem solver, she had the innate ability to rapidly connect disparate elements and make complex matters understandable for clients. The partners, however, saw her as an overachiever with a "take no prisoners" communication style. Ironically, her communicative style that rankled them—of an achievement oriented, skilful problem solver who interprets multiple perspectives—was the very reason the firm had originally recruited Ms. Lin. In my coaching process with her, none of the overly ambitious or aggressive style was evident. In meetings she asked many questions using only a direct communication style. Some thought she asked too many questions or offered too many opposing views. She bantered with colleagues but did not taunt or berate other associates. She was definitely achievement oriented and wanted to find the best solution for her clients. Reading through all of these points, I found she behaved in the same manner as her male colleagues.

In this case, there are culture and gender stereotypes that would hinder the implementation of Sandberg's manifesto. Perceptions became reality for Ms. Lin and eventually impacted her promotion to partner. Joyce Fletcher (2002) calls this a "separate spheres phenomenon," using sex-type attributes to interpret an activity. For example, "A white man slamming his fist on the table during a meeting is perceived quite differently from a man of colour—or any woman—doing the same thing" (2002, 3). Likewise Barack Obama's famous phlegmatic "No Drama Obama" persona may well be a manifestation of not wanting to be perceived as an "angry black man." As Marie Wilson (2007) points out, the same applies to being viewed as ambitious. The mental blueprint also applies across cultures. If we believe someone from one culture should be indirect and self-effacing, observing an opposite behavior disturbs our view and distorts our response.

There are two compelling lessons to add to this discussion. First, our reactions have the potential to teach and change our thinking. I pointed out to the partners that Ms. Lin's strengths were the same attributes displayed by her male colleagues. That may have provided an insight but unfortunately did not change their perspective. In Vietnam my students' adamant rejection of the word ambition and links to leadership taught me a lesson. Initially, I questioned their reactions but eventually understood the implications. Working in multicultural environments offers a powerful learning platform, but only if we are prepared to listen.

Second, the word "ambition" is attributed to individualistic cultures and outdated leadership models. "Contribution" is more relevant to multicultural environments and the new face of leadership. For example, the midcareer Singaporean women favored contribution over ambition. For Ms. Ito and Ms. Ali (although not explicitly stated) this is exactly what they set out to do. Their visions (or in their words "goals") are to benefit the next generation of leaders and the community at large. Interestingly, Sheryl Sandberg and Facebook represent this new face of leadership. The new face of leadership is diverse, creative, and collaborative. Making a contribution fits well as "the very definition of leadership, the rules of the game themselves, will be changed, and are already changing" (Montouri 2010, 7). Rather than more programs for women to learn how to be ambitious, organizations need ways to address systemic issues and mental blueprints that hinder career success. Women usually know where they want to go, but organizations need to rethink attitudes toward female leaders and join in Sandberg's dialogue. The goals are similar; it's the *how* that is different.

Although I do not view the world from a monocultural perspective, I reacted and asked questions from this angle. My weltanschauung has been shaped significantly by my time in Asia, specifically by my years China. Yet, my research in leadership has been influenced by American scholars, James McGregor Burns, Bernard Bass, and Alice Eagly. In retrospect I appraised cultural values—such as face and failure—too quickly and placed judgment on my participants based on an American theory of leadership. If not for the sake of time providing me with the ability to reflect on these stories, cultures, participants, and myself, I would have progressed down a slippery slope of misleading meanings.

My goal was to develop stories based on leadership lessons from the experiences of this cross-cultural group of women. To do so, I needed to confront the false beliefs. I implicitly held about cultures and used to evaluate the intersections between gender and culture and that may have caused me to miss the story completely. My research highlights difficulties leading multicultural teams, and the only solution was to step back and question assumptions and long-held beliefs. Reviewing my interview notes and coming face to face with these uncomfortable feelings was the first step.

How often do we reflect before making decisions about people inside organizations? Narrative inquiry allows the researcher to look inward, outward, backward, and forward. Over distance and time, whether physical or mental, the researcher can unpack feelings, deconstruct knowledge, and explore new ways of knowing. Making quick decisions will seldom benefit narrative research or diverse work environments. Organizations need to look internally at leadership processes, examine the context, and reevaluate frameworks carried forward from previous years. This takes time, deliberation, and awareness.

What Are the Next Steps?

The first step is to build reflexivity into the organizational mindset. The reflexive process moves beyond self-awareness. Reflexivity, originating in the social sciences, links to counseling, research, and economics. Reflexivity is the process of introspection to understand values and experiences that impact decision making, combined with awareness and insights based on an external perspective—how others view us. Reflexivity is bending backward while using an inward and outward approach to review an action, check bias, and learn from the experience.

Reflexivity provides a way to become aware of our culture, recognize the nuances around us, and use this knowledge to better understand decisions. Etherington (2004) states "to be reflexive we need to be *aware* of our personal responses and to be able to make choices about how we use them" (2004, 19). Naturally, it is hard to keep personal instincts in check, but distance provides opportunity for a more informed decision based on experience and context. Interludes provide insights on distortions that often cloud thinking. This means not rushing decisions regarding people, challenging deep-seated beliefs, and being open to accept such challenges.

Reflexivity becomes a critical component of how we see and interpret leadership.

The second step is to learn courage. Courage has been discussed for centuries, from Greek philosophers to religious leaders, as both a virtue and a value. More recently within the positive psychology movement, Christopher Peterson and Martin Seligman (2004) designed the concept of values-in-action, classifying character strengths and aligning vocabulary. While this is a relatively new field of psychology, there's much empirical research underpinning the values project. In their research, Seligman and Peterson found common virtues in multiple cultures, with links to Confucianism, Hinduism, and Islam. One of the core virtues (now classified as strengths) is courage linked with bravery, persistence, integrity, and vitality. I have found few organizations listing courage as a leadership competency although some define courage as a value. Courage sometimes comes under the heading of respect, integrity, or self-awareness, but separating and defining this as a value drives change. Including courage among organizational values moves beyond cursory conversations and into the people processes. More than having a courageous conversation, organizations needs courage to take risks on people, challenge their own thinking, question their beliefs, and change their perspective.

CHAPTER 10

Conclusion: A Roadmap for the Future—What Do We Know?

Leadership is never easy, and today some would say it has never been more difficult. Reviewing the turbulence of the last decade, the future can appear increasingly hazy. The global lament of "Where are the leaders?" combined with more tomes, thought papers, and blogs on leadership can confuse even the most focused. Two significant factors—globalization and technology—have impacted the twenty-first century and redefined our overall perspective and expectations of leadership. To now glean insights of the future means looking around and through these two factors to better understand such complexity and the inevitable contradictions.

Although globalization allows tremendous work diversity, inclusiveness still remains an enigma in many organizations, large and small. And while the advent of technology can blend and homogenize disciplines as well as cultures, it is often the case that many embedded organizational values have not yet changed radically. Not yet. Organizations vacillate, sometimes embracing differences and at other times holding onto outdated leadership models. Predicting the future is almost certainly a fool's errand, but we try nonetheless. It is not hard to see that through increasing globalization and technology, we all are continually nudged to be ever-more adaptable, at a faster clip than we may used to. Throughout this book, we can see a new and different picture of leadership steadily emerging. This particular chapter pulls together insights from four thematic stories, dipping beneath the demographics in order to consider future leadership paradigms.

Peter Drucker (1992) and Raine Eisler (1995) laid the groundwork for challenges faced by today's organizations and leadership. Both called the phase a "period of transformation," bringing new values, reorganizing systems, and reshaping society. Such a transformation is not tied to any one country or continent, it is global, and has to be. The global financial crisis of 2008 would be one example of this transformational phase, and a catalyst behind demographics shifts. As the US economy slowed, Asia blossomed, offering abundant commercial opportunities. Although economic upheaval is one engine of change, technology is also essential in driving change—less dramatic, perhaps, but paramount. Many organizations have reshaped themselves. No longer hierarchies of control, they are more flattened, and can be considered "networks of collaboration." The outdated "dominator model" of power has moved toward partnerships of engagement (Eisler and Montouri 2001, 11).

Correspondingly, employees' values and ways of working have changed. Global organizations are diverse communities of multicultural, multigenerational knowledge workers. However, many organizational mind-sets have not quite caught up with this shift. Most adhere to competency frameworks, with an emphasis on a more transactional, control and command leadership, more germane to an era long gone. Navigating change is never straightforward, and in this period of transformation, achieving any such change will involve setbacks, tension, and periods of dysfunction. Adroit management through this transformational process requires a high degree of intuition and sensitivity, which leads to adroit leadership.

Sizeable Demographic Shifts

To understand the impact of this transformation requires a review of the demographic shifts across Asia. As mentioned, this is a global change, but for the sake of this book, the focus remains Asia. Representing over half of the world's population, Asia increasingly offers channels of growth and opportunities for global organizations. The numbers are staggering. China's modernization plan, for example, requires relocating over 900 million Chinese from the countryside into newly built cities in the next 10–15 years (Miller, T. 2012, Johnson 2013). Nothing on such a scale has ever been attempted. The opportunities for global organizations are enormous, from product distribution to innovation. Consumer spending increases and demand for products rises.

However, challenges persist: this demographic shift and the purported benefits are riddled with contradictions, specifically the supply and demand of professional talent. Peeling back the demographics uncovers a stark reality, starting with India and China, both with over a billion–plus population, multiple megacities, and an educated and noneducated workforce. India and China also have a steady exodus of unskilled workers migrating from agricultural communities toward major metropolitan areas. India's urbanization accounts for 340 million moving into urban centers (Sankhe 2010). This migratory number alone is equal to the population of the United States.

In China, the Central Government's forced relocation started a few years ago, the population living in cities and towns increased to "691 million taking China's ration past 51%" (Miller 2012, 2). Collective farming, impacted by bird flu and other disasters, will be dismantled by urbanization. Historically, moving from agrarian communities to urban centers has been positive for any emerging market economy, but the size and speed in Asia belies the problems. Such an agrarian exodus must be accompanied by investments in education and infrastructure, along with a committed environmental plan. While India's middle class and consumer class spend has increased, national frailties remain. Economic growth guardedly continues, but India has over one third of the world's malnourished children. As technology outsourcing progresses, literacy rates for women are low, with over a half unable to read or write (Luce

2007). Although similar in size, there are stark differences between India and China. Educational reform began under Mao in 1949 and continues today, with an emphasis on science, technology, engineering, and math (STEM; Gao 2013). The Chinese Academy of Science states that women have due representation in the STEM workforce. India presents a different picture, with only 39 percent of women in the workforce, as compared to China's 74 percent (Fincher 2013, Madgavkar 2012). However, this too is inconsistent; the aforementioned 74 percent includes farm workers, no doubt a declining percentage under the wave of mass urbanization (Fincher 2013).

Looking beyond China and India, the rest of Asia presents similar opportunities and challenges. In Southeast Asia, Indonesia, with a quarter of a billion people, has become a slowly rising economic engine. Though rich in natural resources, a growing middle class, and a young workforce with over 55 million skilled workers (Oberman et al. 2012), Indonesia still faces a shortage of professional talent. Like Malaysia, women in Indonesia hold the key to economic development. Japan confronts the same issues from a different perspective. With over 125 million people, Japan struggles with economic reforms, an aging population, and environmental disasters. South Korea has a population of over 50 million, and a somewhat more resilient economy. Yet, in Japan and Korea, the professional working woman remains responsible for child care. Unlike other countries in Asia, where imported labor is more prevalent, Japan's immigration policies preclude such support. Although Japan has a maternity leave policy of up to 58 weeks, day care is in short supply (Ray et al. 2009). Korea expects full participation of women in the workforce, but maintains a hefty gender pay gap. Japan, Korea, Singapore, Vietnam, and Hong Kong, grounded in Confucian values, are often blamed for hindering women's progress. Yet, Singapore and Hong Kong are regional commercial and financial hubs in Asia, both with small populations, and both have a sizeable percentage of women in the workforce. Comparatively, Vietnam has a sizeable percentage of women working and approximately 33% in senior management positions (Grant Thornton 2013). That said, Singapore and Hong Kong trail behind the United States on percentages of women in executive roles. Bangladesh's population is over 150 million, has a strong garment manufacturing base, but a much smaller percentage of women working outside the home. Yet the recent push for girls' education, coupled with garment manufacturing, has increased their participation. Demographics presents a rosy picture until the curtain is drawn back revealing a growing inequality of status, a decline of educational parity, health, and environment concerns. According to John Knapp (2007), "The truth is that we now live in a world in which 2.8 billion people are living on less than two dollars each day, and 1.2 billion are attempting to survive on only one dollar a day" (16).

The percentages of women in the workforce only hint at equalization. Most women still lag sorely behind in terms of compensation and decision-making roles. Globally, women predominate in middle management, ensuring a supply of talent for executive positions. Yet the numbers have not translated into rewards. Women in executive positions remain low, although the percentage of women college graduates has increased. In the United States, women now hold approximately 60 percent of all bachelor degrees. In Asia, the number of women BA graduates fluctuates at around 57 percent (Rosin 2012, McKinsey Research 2012). While women wield considerable economic clout and are responsible for 83 percent of household purchasing decisions, organizations struggle to fully engage this group (Hewlett 2007). In the next five years, organizations will face a shortfall of talent—the rise of lower skilled workers and an increasing retirement of baby boomers. As will be seen in Japan, Malaysia, Indonesia, and Bangladesh, fuller employment of women will thwart this shortfall.

Technology Drives Collectivism and Collaboration

Globalization and technology are inextricably linked. Both have disrupted and permeated every aspect of work and life. Both have social and cultural implications. Both are impartial and unequal. Both factors also benefitted my participants. Demographics aside, technology has driven change at work and in personal lives. Disrupting the traditional 9-to-5 model, work today is anytime and anywhere. Organizations have reaped rich rewards from such efficiencies and reductions in labor costs. Individuals benefit from flexible schedules, but also experience stress from a 24/7 work culture. In my research, participants relied heavily on technology to manage and integrate their lives. Yet not everyone experienced the positive side of technology. Knowledge workers have displaced manual labor, economically hurting some communities more than others.

The rise of social technologies offers ample opportunities for innovation through collaboration. Work shifts from the individual to collective networks. This method of working is similar to the prevailing more collective cultures of Asia: Japan, China, Korea, Hong Kong, Taiwan, Singapore, Malaysia, Indonesia, and India—all emphasize the group, commitment, and trust. Cultures harmonize through these virtual communities. Organizations can learn much from online gaming communities and how these collaborative and inclusive working groups cooperate and innovate (McGonigal 2011). Success in such ventures depends on communication skills, cross-cultural awareness, and creative problem solving. These communities depend on relationships, and they must rely on soft power to defuse conflict. Social technologies have not only reinvented organizations but reframed cross-cultural ways of working as well. While the concept of work-life integration started earlier, the rise of social networks—Facebook and LinkedIn included—fused the separation.

Social networks and online gaming communities represent multiple million memberships. These interdependent communities adapt to the needs of the group. Value is created through interactions and viability through renewal. The new global economy, supported through social technologies, creates interconnected communities, changes communication, and levels the diverse playing field (McGonigal 2011). Two themes stem from this shift: the rise in free agents and the search for meaningful work. It is widely recognized that technology and social networks has given rise to self- employed contractors. Temporary project work (ironically) offers security for the individual, and measureable savings to organizations. Free agents control their destiny, unencumbered by difficult bosses or bureaucratic lumbering. Such desires match the need to find "meaningful work," an increasing chant today among the Millenials. The search for "meaningful work" was, coincidentally, frequently discussed by my participants, often couched under the guise of spirituality, or "seeking purpose."

Meaningful Work, Positive Psychology, and Spirituality

Other than technology, economic shifts and perpetual organizational restructuring bring upheaval, tensions, and a yearning for stability. The rise of the free agent, along with the desire to control one's destiny through a different work template, may be an outcome of this transformation. One of the themes in my research was spirituality. Spirituality—like leadership—is poorly defined. While Ms. Lee linked spirituality with religious affiliation others referred to finding a purpose. Meaning and purpose are part of McKinsey's Centered Leadership Model (Barsh 2008). The vitality in this model reverberates through each capability. It is a holistic approach combining mind, body, and spirituality.

Questions on finding self and purpose typically occur at mid-life. Mid-life is often thought to be the late 30s or the early 40s, but the range differs across cultures. The Millennial Generation does not wait until mid-life; starting a career begins with aligning purpose (Taylor and Keeter 2010). McCann's Truth Series (2012) found that in China, women in their late 20s began this introspective period of self-discovery. Mid-life or mid-career for women is often a reflective period to understand purpose, meaning, and legacy. This self-reflection combined with an external perspective of purpose is the basis of leadership. The significant aspect of this self-reflection is that organizations, typically, lose women at this critical leadership juncture.

Spirituality and purpose coincide with more than the age of transformation—this value cuts across time and cultures. Along with the finding of meaning is the rise in positive psychology. Martin Seligman is known as the originator of this movement. Positive psychology is a scientific movement grounded in mental health research, reframing the focus on ailments to a discussion on well-being. Before Seligman, Victor Frankl developed a similar approach in psychotherapy and the search for meaning (Pink 2005). Frankl believed that "man's search for meaning is a primary motivation in his life, not a secondary rationalization of instinctual drives" (Frankl 1992, 105). Positive psychology uncovers meaning through quantitative research on virtues, strengths, and weaknesses. Both Seligman and Frankl remain focused on human potential and the leading of a purposeful life. Seligman's theory was influenced by Maslow's hierarchy of needs. Maslow believed that the individual's move through various stages to reach potential could ultimately achieve true self-actualization. Although highly criticized, using contemporary terms of Maslovian theory has clear applications to organizations, leadership, and individual needs. Self-actualization is now defined as creative problem solving, acceptance, and morality. Richard Barrett (1998) in his book, *Liberating the Corporate Soul*, developed a similar organizational model, predicting future organizations would have flexible structures, meaningful jobs, and a greater concern with spiritual health. This sounds remarkably familiar to the current realities.

Both positive psychologists and leadership researchers have focused on character and the moral good (Peterson and Seligman 2004, Knapp 2007). For my participants, spirituality, meaningful work, and leadership for the greater good were easily discernible:

- Ms. Lee regularly discussed her spiritual beliefs, which were linked to her religious affiliation, and she spent time coaching women from her church community.
- Ms. Ito defined spirituality in her work. This came through in her quest to end poverty and hunger.
- Ms. Ali discussed spirituality not in terms of religion but in terms of doing meaningful work, leadership defined by being of service to those you are leading.
- Ms. Chin's fundamental values were trust and respect. Without these, she does not think anyone can lead.

The economic and technological disruptions have catapulted the shift toward positive psychology and values-based leadership. Seligman and Peterson examined character, using six virtues in individuals, industries, cultures, and institutions. One virtue, now called values, is courage, which they defined as persistence, having the determination to (ethically) achieve against all odds. Concurrently, research of "good" leaders found excellence, ethics, and meaningful engagement (Knapp 2007). Besides character, moral values inside organizations and with leaders can be a catalyst for change. To wit, Gandhi's moral power to change a nation, or Barack Obama's moral values underpinning foreign policy, which can be interpreted as vacillation or weakness, others calling it deliberate, steady, and ethical. While similarities between the two theories are strong, their alignment with my participants is uncanny. Reflecting on the interviews, their stories share the same drive toward excellence and the determination to achieve, keeping ethics intact.

Seligman's value of courage links to my participants' discussion on determination. Like integrity, determination was easily seen in each of them. There is a treasure trove of research indicating that women try harder—and believe they must *always* try harder (than male counterparts) to succeed, a tactical effort rather than a strategic one. As discussed in this book, women *are* viewed differently and *do* face different challenges. Therefore determination and persistence to achieve make sense. Determination is interestingly not ranked highly among leadership qualities. Kouzes and Posner (2003) surveyed values across cultures and found approximately only 30 percent of the respondents ranked determination as an admired characteristic of leaders. In defining "determination" some leadership texts connect the words "dominance, directing, and assertiveness." However, dominance and directing may not resonate cross-culturally. Honesty, competency, and inspirational are ranked higher.

My participants' stories depict a strong determination and capacity to overcome obstacles. Determination became a powerful force to overcome both invisible and structural barriers. Ms. Ali's ability to reduce negative stereotypes associated with Islam became a driving force for good. Ms. Ito's determination to make a difference was realized through the organization, redirecting revenue to solve social problems. Ms. Ito and Ms. Ali distanced themselves physically and emotionally from family in order to become the leaders they are today. Ms. Lee persisted against the odds in both Africa and China, overcoming a narcissistic leader and organizational chaos. Ms. Chin's hard work allowed her to seize opportunity, and her previous participation on a winning sports team underscored her determination to achieve.

Personal challenges, pivotal moments, and renewal provided a path to leadership. My participants' determination became an ability to endure, with the tenacity to succeed. Authenticity and a foundation of ethics permeated every story. This ethical fiber connects all of them. Through this discussion, the era of financial malfeasance—or the leader as charismatic hero—begins to fade. The quest for meaningful work, the determination to achieve, and morally good leaders provide the foundation for future leadership models.

Networks, Integrating Work and Life

Marie Wilson states, "The capacity for community building is one of the significant factors increasing the odds that women will lead" (Rhodes and Kellerman 2007, 275). A salient feature from this research is the act of building a connected, inclusive web to sustain success. This way of working moves over and across cultures and generations, similar to how an organization operates. Ms. Chin's centered connected approach, matching work groups, family, sport teams, board activities, and social groups is uniquely Asian. Similarly, Cheung and Halpern (2008) found executive women with a similar strategy and a preference for integrating all aspects of their lives. They also uncovered sequencing, taking time off from their careers to focus on family and eventually returning to work. However, such a career strategy did not always work or pay off.

As a traditional Chinese axiom states, "one is nothing without the group." Ms. Chin's inclusive network resembled a spider web of connections, of which an important element is maintaining harmony. While some may now claim cultural values are merging, this value of harmony remains embedded in many Asian cultures. Harmony goes back to the tenets of Taoism and Confucianism, and harmony also connects with the use of soft power to manage diverse relationships. Ms. Chin shared insights on how this web maintained harmony between various groups all competing for her time. Although my other participants did not describe it in the same level of detail, all shared similar stories, building on the concept of this web of inclusion.

The term "web of inclusion" was first mentioned by Sally Helgesen (1995) in her book *The Female Advantage*. She discussed how women lead from the center, solidly placed in the *middle* of the organization, rather than the top. "In the web construction the figurehead is the heart rather than the head, and so does not need layers and ranks below to reinforce status. Authority comes from connection to the people around rather than distance from those below; this in itself helps foster a team approach" (55).

Ms Chin described the same positioning. Standing in the middle of her office, Ms. Chin was surrounded by a solid team of high performers. More than the team, she made it a point to include her (extended) family and sports community, all interconnected. Helgesen presents a fluid, renewable web that is "guided by opportunity, proceeds by intuition, and is characterized by patience that comes from waiting to see what comes next" (1995, 59).

My participants described a different format, driven by efficiencies rather than opportunities. The web facilitated opportunities, specifically new positions, or helped navigate obstacles. Given the determined spirit of my participants, except for Ms. Ito, the "waiting to see what comes next" is not something they would easily entertain. Sharp lines and rigid charts no longer apply; organizations are virtual networks of relationships. There have always been influential organizational networks but they are now more observable, vocal, and pronounced. These networks of relationships move away from the individual toward the group.

This connected web aligns with collective cultures the group rather than makes the individual stand out. In addition, the web accepts diversity and embraces inclusion. There is no one "right" way to deliver, as multiple perspectives are considered. This is not to say, democracy drives every decision. The point is, the web offers a model of inclusiveness. For organizations struggling to become inclusive, operating across this relationship network weaves different voices and diverse perspectives together.

If technology is the force reducing hierarchy, social technology is the power engine supporting networked organizations. Both support this integrated web. This has not reduced complexity; organizations still operate across multiple cultures through virtual and physical collaborative communities. Knowledge workers remain, but social networks and online gaming have moved this group to the next dimension. This interconnected virtual community collaborates to achieve mutual goals. The focus is on engaging these diverse groups through meaningful work. The next generation of leadership will have to come from these multicultural and multigenerational work groups.

Cross-Cultural Relevancy

In a world of social media where everybody is connected to every-one through social networks, gaming communities, or information systems, the concept of cultural differences becomes less relevant, or at least needs redefinition. Conducting this research across multiple cultures raised questions on identity and location of culture. The cultural comparison dialogue is out of date and reflects a hegemonic monologue reflective of the colonial and postcolonial world (Bhabha 1994, Probyn 1996, Ong 1995). The discussion aligned with con-temporary organizations and leadership now shifts to identity, a far more complex and relevant topic. This research addressed multicul-turalism and the multiple identities women assume: wife, mother, daughter, professional, and leader.

Stacilee Ford, in her book *Troubling American Women* draws insights from composite stories of Americans, Europeans, and Chinese Americans who lived in Hong Kong and Macao (Ford 2011). The book highlights cultural challenges, gender myths, and issues of national identity. The ongoing negotiation between cultures moves beyond national mind-sets toward a "rubber-band nationality" (Ford 2011, 155), stretching and shrinking through cultures—as did my participants. As a researcher, I too experienced a personal shrinking and stretching between my America-centric views, mindful of my location and participants. Cross-cultural narrative is an expansive archaeological dig, years of patient unearthing, often having to move from one location to another repeatedly. The motivation for using stories was to bring culture, gender, and the unheard voice to the forefront. Stories are learning tools that provide insight into the expansive subject of leadership. Through my participants, digging deeper into their experiences, I uncovered the art of listening and reflexivity (Davies et al. 2004). Their stories led to moments of realization for them, for me, and for leadership.

Leadership for the Future

Leadership is connected, providing guidance, coaching, and sup-port. The participative attributes of transformational leaders fit well. More than managing an exchange, leaders move up Maslow's hierarchy of needs actively engaging followers to achieve outcomes. Transactional management, focused on exchange and reward, seldom fits more nimble or contemporary organizations. The intrinsic reward within the newer collective communities is not reliant on individual achievement. Personal growth and reward comes from developing a unique product or solving an insurmountable problem within the community (McGonigal 2011).

The last decade has been a zigzag of economic change and an exposure of leadership failures, political and commercial. When the United States defaulted, Asia blossomed. Asia will continue to bloom, with inevitable periods of disruption. Leadership will move from a "hero" competency model toward a more ethical foundation. Ethics is, and will continue to be, at the heart of leadership (Ciulla, 2004). In an era of change and chaos, leadership will be tested, and spirituality will find a place in commerce.

At the core of leadership are relationships. At the center of these diverse relationships is trust and integrity. While multinationals rank "global mind-sets" at the top of leadership characteristics, the second value is integrity. Trust and integrity have been compromised in the past couple of decades. The increase in books, research, and assessments to measure "trust" in organizations supports this assertion. Edelman, a global public relations firm, conducts an annual survey of trust across multiple industries and countries. This is the largest global survey on trust, and in 2013 the focus was on leadership trust.

Similarly, Thomson Reuters conducts a trust index, concentrating on the health and climate within the financial industry. The World Economic Forum administers a global opinion survey with more than 20,000 participants in over 20 countries. Past surveys revealed "an alarming picture of declining levels of trust" (Knapp 2007, 34). Surveys post-2008 reveal a similar picture but with some uptake on the positive side for industries. There is not only a global deficit of trust, there's also a question of "trust" with the actual surveys. Some of the distrust may come from the emotional attachment to the word, the connections to relationships, and with leadership (Solomon 2004). Recent bank failures, accounting scandals, tainted food products, lack of data privacy, and such have all accounted for the deficit of trust in both the public and private sectors globally. And once again, this points back to leadership.

For my participants, integrity was the first point from these stories. Trust was a close second often embedded in the stories on relationships. More than mere storytelling, Ms. Ito, Ms. Ali, Ms. Lee, and Ms. Chin provided leadership experiences from distinctly different industries and cultures. The narrative supported both my intellectual and emotional journey to learn from these women. Along the way, I uncovered poignant childhood events, political unrest, incurable disease, and tragedy, providing a somewhat convoluted path with complicated plots and changing storylines. The stories started on a linear path but turned upside down, back-and-forth—exploring words, notes, and renewing the narrative. Looking back, three themes surfaced: determination, spirituality, and an integrated web. Instead of being prescriptive or creating another model of leadership, these three themes are mapped against global trends running through organizations. Rereading my notes and writing down these stories provided a new perspective on how Asian Women Lead.

Reflecting on what I heard, these women are morally upright leaders, with the self-determination and courage to make a difference in the world. The second half of this study grapples with leadership theory. While the definition of leadership remains elusive, John Knapp believes leadership in the future "requires a renewed commitment to listening, speaking honestly, acting with integrity, and seeking outcomes that serve the best interest of all" (2007, 40). To this point, I would add the ability to listen reflexively. If one point stood out while conducting this study, it was reflexivity. The ability to look back on one's self is seen throughout this study. This is increasingly important for leadership, critical for narrative, and crucial in uncovering bias.

My research and work are interconnected; both fuel a relentless pursuit to understand leadership experiences through the voice of the individual from a multicultural perspective. This research has become a transformative journey, capturing snippets of lives with each story to learn from these experiences (Bochner 2000). Writing stories from many angles and methods offers a new perspective on my participants, on narrative inquiry, and women leaders. What crystallized for me were moments of realization, epiphanies that drove them to action. These actions were very different from that of their peers. The book intends to expand knowledge of cross-cultural leadership based on stories around culture with participants in the intersection of work and life. It began with a fictionalized voice of Mitchy, a cross-cultural business leader. That story is true, but the character and events were changed. The book's intent is to interact with the content, reread, and discover something new. To draw a plausible conclusion means the reader must be comfortable with the narrative and the continuous learning journey. As is true with life, a story changes with each reading.

Hanna Rosin (2012) in her book *The End of Men* states, "Asian women will take over the world" (2012, 231). Looking at demographics, she might be right. More than numbers, working collaboratively utilizes women's strengths in transformational leadership. There are noticeably fewer women in decision-making roles in Asia, but organizations and governments are working to build balance. Asia offers phenomenal opportunities along with contradictions and complexities. The only constant is change. The frenzied pace of change will not abate and economic disruptions will continue. Organizations need to develop leaders, not leadership models. In order to do so, they need a new lens to see this talented group of women. The prevailing, dominant leadership model should be tossed out with a return to values and ethics. If the past is any indication, the trends shaping the workforce positively reinforce women's leadership strengths.

REFERENCES

Adler, N. J. 1997. Global Leadership: Women Leaders, Management International Review. *International Human Resource and Cross-Cultural Management* 37: 171–196.

Agger, B. 1991. Critical Theory, Poststructuralism, Postmodernism: Their Sociological Relevance. *Annual Review Social* 17: 105–131.

Aguirre, D., and J. Sabbagh. 2010. The Third Billion. *Strategy and Business* 59: 1–3.

Ahmed, S. 2004. *Bangladesh Past and Present.* New Delhi: APH Publishing.

Ammeter, A., C. Douglas, W. L. Gard, W. A. Hochwarer, and G. R. Ferris. 2002. Toward a Political Theory of Leadership. *The Leadership Quarterly* 13: 751–796.

Andrews, M. 2007. Exploring Cross-Cultural Boundaries. In *Handbook of Narrative Inquiry*, edited by D. J. Clandinin, 489–511. Thousand Oaks, CA: Sage.

Armitage, S., and S. Gluck. 2002. Reflections on Women's Oral History: An Exchange. In *Women's Oral History: The Frontiers Reader*, edited by S. H. Armitage, P. Hart, and K. Weatherman, 73–82. Lincoln: University of Nebraska.

Avery, D. 2011. Support for Diversity at Organizations: A Theoretical Explanation of its Origins and Offshoots. *Organizational Psychology Review* 1 (3): 239–256.

Avolio B. J., and W. Gardner. 2005. Authentic Leadership Development: Getting to the Root of Positive Forms of Leadership. *The Leadership Quarterly* 16: 315–338.

Baddeley, S., and K. James. 1987. Owl, Fox, Donkey, or Sheep: Political Skills for Managers. *Management Learning* 87 (3): 3–19.

Bangladesh Out of the Basket. 2012. *The Economist,* November 3–9.

Barnes, J. 1984. *Flaubert's Parrot* London: Picador.

Barrett R. 1998. Liberating the Corporate Soul: Building a Visionary Organisation. Boston: Butterworth Heinemann.

Barry, E. 1973. *Robert Frost on Writing.* New Brunswick, NJ: Rutgers University Press.

Barsh, J., S. Devillard, and J. Wang. 2012. The Global Gender Agenda. *McKinsey Quarterly,* November, 1–11.

Barsh, J., and L. Yee. 2011. Changing Companies' Minds About Women. *McKinsey Quarterly* September, 1–11.

Barsh, J., S. Cranston, and R. Craske. 2008. Centered Leadership: How Talented Women Thrive. *McKinsey Quarterly* 4 (November): 36–48.

Bass, B. M. 1995. Theory of Transformational Leadership Redux. *Leadership Quarterly* 6 (4): 463–478.

Bass, B. M. 1999. On The Taming of Charisma: A Reply to Janice Beyer. *Leadership Quarterly* 10 (4): 541–553.

Bass, B. M., and P. Steidlmeier. 2004. Ethics, Character, and Authentic Transformational Leadership Behavior. In *Ethics, the Heart of Leadership,* edited by Joanne Ciulla, 175–196. Westport, CT: Praeger Publishers.

Bateson, M. C. 2000. *Full Circles, Overlapping Lives: Culture and Generation in Transition.* New York: Random House.

Behar R., and D. Gordon, eds. 1995. *Women Writing Culture.* Los Angeles: University of California Press.

Bennett, C. 2010. *Muslim Women of Power: Gender Politics and Culture in Islam.* New York, Continuum.

Bergsten, C. F., C. Freeman, N. R. Lardy, and D. J. Mitchell. 2008. *China's Rise: Challenges and Opportunities.* Washington, D.C.: Peterson Institute for International Relations Center for Strategic Studies.

Bhabha, H. 1994. *The Location of Culture.* London: Routledge.

Bhatti, K. 2011/2012. The Birth of Bangladesh. *Socialism Today* 154, December–January. Retrieved August 29, 2011, from http://www.socialismtoday.org/154/bangladesh.html.

Bochner, A. 2000. Criteria Against Ourselves. *Qualitative Inquiry* 6 (2): 266–272.

Bolman, L. G., and T. E. Deal. 2008. *Reframing Organizations: Artistry, Choice, and Leadership.* 4th ed. San Francisco: Jossey-Bass.

Bolden R., and J. Gosling. 2006 Leadership Competencies: Time to Change the Tune? *Leadership* 2 147–163.

Bond, M. 1991. *Beyond the Chinese Face: Insights from Psychology.* Hong Kong: Oxford University Press.

Bowles, H. R., and L. C. Babcock. 2008. When Doesn't it Hurt Her to Ask? *Framing and Justification Reduce the Social Risks of Initiating Compensation.* IACM 21st Annual Conference Paper. Retrieved August 10, 2011, from or http://dx.doi.org/10.2139/ssrn.1316162.

Bowles, H. R., L. Babcock, and L. Lai. 2007. Social Incentives for Gender Differences in the Propensity to Initiate Negotiations: Sometimes It Does Hurt to Ask. *Organizational Behavior and Human Decision Processes* 103 (1): 84–103.

Bowles, H., and K. McGuinn. 2005. Claiming Authority Negotiating Challenges for Women Leaders. In *The Psychology of Leadership New Perspectives and Research,* edited by D. Messick and R. Kramer, 191–208. Mahwah, NJ: Lawrence Erlbaum.

Bowles, H., and K. McGuinn. 2008. Gender in Job Negotiations. *Negotiation Journal* 24 (4): 393–410.

Brandon R., and M. Seldman. 2004. *Survival of the Savvy: High Integrity Political Tactics for Career and Company Success.* New York: Free Press.

Brown, B. 2004. *Women and Shame: Reaching Out, Speaking Truth and Building Connection.* Austin, TX: 3C Press.

Brown, A. D., and C. Rhodes. 2005. Writing Responsibly: Narrative Fiction and Organization Studies. *Organization* 12 (4): 505–529.

Buchanan, D. A., and R. J. Badham. 2008. *Power, Politics, and Organizational Change: Winning the Turf War.* 2d ed. London: Sage Publications.

Buck, M. A. 2007. Discovering the Transformative Learning Potential in the Spirituality of Midlife Women. In *Transformative Learning Issues of Differences and Diversity, Seventh International Transformative Learning Conference,* edited by P. Cranton and E.Taylor, 65–70.

Burns, J. M. 2010. *Leadership.* New York, NY : Harper and Row.

Buruma, I. 1984. *A Japanese Mirror: Heroes and Villains of Japanese Culture.* London: Vintage.

Buruma, I. 1989. *God's Dust: A Modern Asian Journey.* London: Vintage.

Buruma, I. 1996. *The Missionary and the Libertine: Love and War in East and West.* London: Faber.

Carter, H. M., v. Hewlett Packard Company. 2010. Class Action Complaint.

Cheung, F., and D. Halpern. 2008. *Women at the Top: Powerful Leaders Tell Us How to Combine Work and Family.* Maldin, MA: Wiley.

Cheung F., and D. Halpern. 2010. Women at the Top: Powerful Leaders Define Success as Work and Family in a Culture of Gender. *American Psychologist* 65 (3): 182–193.

Chhokar, J. S., R. House, and F. C. Brodbeck. 2008. Culture and Leadership Across the World. *The Globe Book on Indepth Studies of 25 Societies.* London: Taylor and Francis.

Chin, J. L., B. Lott, J. Rice, and J. Sanchez-Hucles. 2007. *Women and Leadership: Transforming Visions and Diverse Voices.* Maldin, MA: Blackwell Publishing.

Ciulla, J. B., ed. 2004. *Ethics: The Heart of Leadership.* Westport, CT: Praeger Publishers.

Clandinin, J., and M. Connelly. 1990. Stories of Experience and Narrative Inquiry. *Educational Researcher* 19 (5): 2–14.

Clandinin, J., and M. Connelly. 2000. *Narrative Inquiry: Experience and Story in Qualitative Research.* London: Jossey Bass.

Clandinin, D. J., and J. Huber. 2010. Narrative Inquiry. In *International Encyclopedia of Education,* 3d ed., edited by B. McGaw, E. Baker, and P. P. Peterson, 1–26. New York: Elsevier.

Clandinin, D. J., D. Pushor, and A. Or. 2007. Navigating Sites for Narrative Inquiry. *Journal of Teacher Education* 58 (1): 21–35.

Clough, P. 2002. *Narrative and Fictions in Educational Research* Oxford: Open University Press.

Coben, H. 2009. *Tell No One.* New York: Dell.

Coben, H. 2011. *Live Wire.* New York: Dutton.

Coffee, A., and P. Atkinson. 1996. *Making Sense of Qualitative Data: Complementary Research Strategies.* Thousand Oaks, CA: Sage.

Coffman, J., O. Gadish, and W. Miller. 2010. The Great Disappearing Action: Gender Parity Up The Corporate Ladder. *Bain Study,* 1–11. Davos: Bain & Company.

Conger, J. A. 1999. Charismatic and Transformational Leadership in Organizations: An Insider's Perspective on these Developing Streams of Research. *Leadership Quarterly* 10 (2): 145–179.

Coughlin, L., E. Wingard, and K. Hollihan. 2005. *Enlightened Power: How Women Are Transforming the Practice of Leadership.* San Francisco: Jossey-Bass.

Culbert, S., and L. Rout 2010. *Get Rid of Performance Reviews! How Companies Can Stop Intimidating and Start Managing and Focus on What Really Matters.* New York: Business Plus.

Davies, C. A. 1999. *Reflexive Ethnography: A Guide to Researching Selves and Others.* London: Routledge.

Davies, B., J. Brown, S. Gannon, E. Honan, C. Laws, B. Mueller-Roshtoch, and E. Peterson. 2004. The Ambivalent Practices of Reflexivity. *Qualitative Inquiry* 10 (3): 360–389.

Dawley, D., J. Hoffman, and A. Smith. 2004. Leadership Succession: Does Gender Matter? *Leadership and Organizational Development Journal* 25 (8): 678–690.

Debarry, T., W. T. Chan, R. J. Lufrano, and J. Adler. 2011. *Sources of Chinese Tradition,* vol. 11. New York : Columbia University Press.

Densten, I., and J. Gray. 2001. Leadership Development and Reflection: What is the Connection? *International Journal of Educational Management* 15 (3): 119–124.

Dent, E., M. E. Higgins, and D. Wharff. 2005. Spirituality and Leadership: An Empirical Review of Definitions, Distinctions, and Embedded Assumptions. *Leadership Quarterly* 16: 625–653.

Denzin, N. 1997. *Interpretive Ethnography: Ethnographic Practice for the Twenty-First Century.* Thousand Oaks, CA: Sage.

Denzin, N., 2000. Aesthetics and Practices of Qualitative Inquiry. *Qualitative Inquiry* 6 (2): 256–265.

Denzin, N., and Y. Lincoln, eds. 2005. *The Sage Handbook of Qualitative Research.* 3d ed. Thousand Oaks, CA: Sage.

Derrida, J. 1978. *Writing and Difference.* London: Routledge.

Dorfman, P., J. Howell, S. Hibono, J. Lee, U. Tate, and A. Bautista, 1997. Leadership in Western and Asian Countries: Commonalities and Differences in Effectiveness Leadership Process Across Cultures. *Leadership Quarterly* 8 (3): 233–274.

Drucker, P. (1992) 2006. The New Society of Organisations. In *Classic Drucker: Essential Wisdom of Peter Drucker from the Pages of Harvard Business Review.* New York: Perseus.

Dyck, I., J. M. Lynam, and J. M. Anderson. 1995. Women Talking: Creating Knowledge Through Difference. *Cross-Cultural Research Women's Studies International Forum* 18 (5/6): 611–626.

Dyckerhoff, C., J. Wang, and J. Chen. 2012. Women Matter: An Asian Perspective Harnessing Female Talent to Raise Corporate Performance. *McKinsey Quarterly,* June.

Eagly, A. H. 2007. Female Leadership Advantage and Disadvantage: Resolving the Contradictions. *Psychology of Women Quarterly* 31: 1–12.

Eagly A. H., and L. Carli, 2003. The Female Leadership Advantage: An Evaluation of the Evidence. *Leadership Quarterly* 14: 807–834.

Eagly, A. H., and L. Carli. 2007. *Through the Labyrinth: The Truth about How Women Become Leaders.* Boston, MA: Harvard University Press.

Eagly, A. H., and M. Johannesen-Schmidt. 2001. The Leadership Styles of Men and Women. *Journal of Social Issues* 57 (4): 781–797.

Eagly, A. H., M. Johannesen-Schmidt, and M. van Engen. 2003. Transformational, Transactional, and Laissez-faire Leadership Styles: A Meta-Analysis Comparing Women and Men. *Psychological Bulletin* 129 (4): 569–591.

Eagly, A. H., and A. Mladinic. 1995. Are People Prejudiced Against Women? Some Answers from Research on Attitudes, Gender Stereotypes, and Judgments of Competence. *European Review of Social Psychology* 5 (1): 1–35.

Earley, C. P., S. Ang, and J. S. Tan. 2006. *CQ: Developing Cultural Intelligence at Work.* Stanford, CA: Stanford University Press.

Ehsan, M. 2002. Moving Towards Miracle: Transferability of Japanese-Style Management in Bangladesh: Rhetoric or Reality? *Asia Affairs* 24 (4): 16–43.

Eisler, R. (1995) 2011. *The Chalice and the Blade: Our History, Our Future.* 1st ed. New York: Harper Collins.

Eisler, R. 2005. The Economics of the Enlightened Use of Power. In *Enlightened Power: How Women are Transforming the Practice of Leadership,* edited by L. Coughlin, E. Wingard, and K. Hollihan, 21–38. San Francisco: Jossey Bass.

Eisler, R., and A. Montouri. 2001. The Partnership Organisation: A Systems Approach. *OD Practioner* 33: 2, 11–17.

Ellis, C., and A. P. Bochner. 2003. Autoethnography, Personal Narrative, Reflexivity: Researcher as Subject. In *Collecting and Interpreting Qualitative Materials,* 2d ed., edited by N. Denzin and Y. S. Lincoln, 199–258. Thousand Oaks, CA: Sage.

Ely, R. J., H. Ibarra, and D. Kolb. 2011. Taking Gender Into Account: Theory and Design for Women's Leadership Programs. *Academy of Management Learning and Education* 10 (3): 2–51.

Ely, R., and D. Myerson. 2000. Theories of Gender: A New Approach to Organisational Analysis and Change. *Research in Organisational Behaviour* 22: 103–155.

Etherington, K. 2004. *Becoming a Reflexive Researcher: Using Our Selves in Research.* London: Kingsley Publishers.

Etherington, K. 2006. Reflexivity: Using our "Selves" in Narrative Research. In *Narrative Research on Learning: Comparative and International Perspectives,* edited by S. Trahar, 77–91. Cambridge: Cambridge University Press.

Ettus, S. 2012. Five Ways to Close the Ambition Gap for Girls. *Forbes.* http://www.forbes.com/sites/samanthaettus/2012/02/02/sheryl-sandberg/.

Fairbank, J. 1992. *China: A New History.* Boston, MA: Harvard University Press.

Fincher Hong, L. 2012 China's Left Over Women. *New York Times,* October 11, http://www.nytimes.com/2012/10/12/opinion/global/chinas-leftover-women.html.

Finder, J. 2008. *Power Play.* New York: St. Martin's Press.

Finlay, L. 2002. Negotiating the Swamp: The Opportunity and Challenge of Reflexivity in Research Practice. *Qualitative Research* 2 (2): 209–230.

Finlay, L. 2006. "Rigour," "Ethical Integrity," or "Artistry"? Reflexively Reviewing Criteria for Evaluating Qualitative Research. *British Journal of Occupational Therapy* 69 (7): 319–326.

Fleschenberg, A. 2009. Some Introductory Reflections. In *Society, Spirituality, and the Sacred: A Social Scientific Introduction*, 2d ed., edited by D. Swenson, ix–xix. Toronto: University of Toronto Press.

Fletcher, J. 2002. The Greatly Exaggerated Demise of Heroic Leadership: Gender, Power, and the Myth of the Female Advantage. *Center for Gender in Organisations.* Briefing Note 13.

Ford, S. 2011. *Troubling American Women: Narratives of Gender and Nation in Hong Kong.* Hong Kong: Hong Kong University Press.

Francesco, A., and S. Mahtani. 2011. Gender Diversity Benchmark for Asia: China, India, Japan, Singapore. In *Diversity and Inclusion in Asia Network Community Business,* March. Retrieved on August 15, 2011, from http://www.communitybusiness.org/images/cb/publications/2011/GDBM_2011.pdf.

Frankl, V. 1992. *Man's Search for Meaning: An Introduction to Logotherapy.* 4th ed. Boston: Beacon Press.

Fu, P. P., R. Wu, and Y. Yang. 2008. Chinese Culture and Leadership. In *Culture and Leadership Across The World: The Globe Book on Indepth Studies of 25 Societies,* edited by Jahdeep Singh Chhokar, Robert House, and Felix C. Brodbeck, 877–907. London: Taylor and Francis.

Fu, P. P., and C. Tsui. 2003. Utilizing Printed Media to Understand Desired Leadership Attributes in the People's Republic of China. *Asia Pacific Journal of Management* 20: 423–446.

Gao, Y. 2013. Report on China's STEM System. Consultant Report Securing Australia's Future. *STEM: Country Comparisons Center for the Study of Higher Education.* University of Melbourne.

Gardner, H. 1995, 2010. *Leading Minds: An Anatomy of Leadership.* New York: Basic Books.

Giordano, J., M. O'Reily, H. Taylor, and N. Dogra. 2007. Confidentiality and Autonomy: The Challenge(s) of Offering Research Participants a Choice of Disclosing Their Identity. *Quality Health Research* 17 (2): 264–275.

Goffman, E. 1959. *The Presentation of Self in Everyday Life.* New York: Anchor.

Goleman, D. 1998. *Working with Emotional Intelligence.* London: Bloomsbury.

Gorelick, S. 1991. Contradictions of Feminist Methodology. *Gender and Society* 5 (4): 459–477.

Grant, Thornton. 2013. *Women in Senior Management: Setting the Stage for Growth.* Grant Thornton International Business Report, 1–2.

Hall, E. T. 1989. *Beyond Culture.* New York: Doubleday.

Hamdan, A. 2009. Narrative Inquiry as a Decolonizing Method. *Interactions: UCLA Journal of Education and Information Studies* 5 (2): 1–20.

Hanley, C. 2005. Beset by Bay's Killer Storms, Bangladesh Prepares and Hopes. *Los Angeles Times,* February 27. Retrieved August 15, 2011, from http://articles.latimes.com/2005/feb/27/news/adfg-bangla27.

Hargrave, D. 2006. Stories of Women's Mid-Life Experience. Master's thesis, University of South Africa.

Harstock, N. 2004. The Feminist Standpoint Developing Ground for Specifically Feminist Historical Materialism. In *The Feminist Standpoint Theory Reader: Intellectual and Political Conversations,* edited by S. Harding, 35–55. New York: Routledge.

He, M. F. 2002. A Narrative Inquiry of Cross Cultural Lives: Lives in Canada. *Journal of Curriculum Studies* 34 (3): 323–342.

Heifetz, R. 2007. Leadership, Authority, and Women. In *Women and Leadership: The State of Play and Strategies for Change,* edited by B. Kellerman and D. Rhode, 311–327. San Francisco: Jossey Bass.

Helgesen, S. 1995. *The Female Advantage: Women's Ways of Leadership.* New York: Doubleday.

Herbert, B. 2006. Hillary Can Run, But Can She Win? *New York Times,* May 18. Retrieved August 15, 2011, from http://www.nytimes.com/2006/05/18/opinion/18herbert.html?_r=0.

Hewlett, S. A. 2007. *Off-Ramps and On-Ramps: Keeping Talented Women on the Road to Success.* Boston, MA: Harvard University Press.

Hewlett, S. A., and R. Rashid. 2011. *Winning the War for Talent in Emerging Markets: Why Women are the Solution.* Boston, MA: Harvard University Press.

Hirschmann, N. 1997. The Feminist Standpoint as Postmodern Strategy. In *Politics and Feminist Standpoint Theories,* edited by S. Kinney and H. Kinsella, 73–92. Philadelphia: Haworth Press.

Hofstede, G., and M. Bond. 1984. Hofstede Dimension of Culture: An Independent Validation Using Rokeach's Value Survey. *Cross-Cultural Psychology* 15 (4): 417–433.

Horan, J. 2011. *I Wish I'd Known That Earlier in My Career: The Power of Positive Workplace Politics.* Singapore: Wiley.

Horan, J. 2012. Words Collide, Mindsets Remain. In *Contextualizing Narrative Inquiry: Developing Methodological Approaches for Local Contexts,* edited by Sheila Trahar, 179–194. London, UK: Routledge.

House, R. J., P. J. Hanges, M. Javidan, P. Dorfman, and V. Gupta, eds. 2004. *Leadership, Culture, and Organisations: The GLOBE Study of 62 Societies.* 1st ed. Thousand Oaks, CA: Sage.

Howard, S. 2002. A Spiritual Perspective on Learning in the Workplace. *Journal of Managerial Psychology* 17 (3): 230–242.

Howard, A., and R. Wellins. 2008/9. *Holding Women Back. Troubling Discoveries and Best Practices for Helping Leaders Succeed.* A Special Report from DDI's Global Leadership Forecast.

Hussain, M. G., and M. A. Mohideen. 2010. *Leadership Styles and Shura System: An Islamic Perspective.* New Delhi: Deep and Deep Publications.

Ibarra, H. 2005. Our Many Possible Selves: What Do We Want? In *Enlightened Power: How Women are Transforming the Practice of Leadership,* edited by L. Coughlin, E. Wingard, and K. Hollihan, 199–261. San Francisco: Jossey Bass.

Ifekwunigwe, J. O. 1999. *Scattered Belongings: Cultural Paradoxes of "Race," Nation, and Gender.* New York: Routledge.

James, K., and T. Arroba. 2005. Reading and Carrying: A Framework for Learning about Emotion and Emotionality. *Management Learning* 36 (3): 299–316.

Johnson, I. 2013. Pitfalls Abound in China's Push from Farm to City. *New York Times*, July 13, http://www.nytimes.com/2013/07/14/world/asia/pitfalls-abound-in-chinas-push-from-farm-to-city.html?pagewanted=all.

Josselson, R., ed. 1996. *Ethics and Process in the Narrative Studies of Lives.* Vol. 4. London: Sage.

Josselson, R. 2006. Narrative Research and the Challenge of Accumulating Knowledge. *Narrative Inquiry* 16 (1): 3–10.

Josselson, R. 2007. The Ethical Attitude in Narrative Research, Principles, and Practice. In *Handbook of Narrative Inquiry,* edited by D. J. Clandinin, 538–566. Thousand Oaks, CA: Sage.

Jung, D. I., and B. Avolio. 1999. Effects of Leadership Style and Follower's Cultural Orientation on Performance in Groups and Individual Task Conditions. *Academy of Management Journal* 42 (2): 208–218.

Kaiser, R. 2009. *The Perils of Accentuating the Positive.* Tulsa, OK: Hogan Press.

Kandola, B. 2009. *The Value of Difference: Eliminating Bias in Organisations.* Oxford: Pearn Kandola Publishing.

Kellerman, B., and D. Rhode. 2007. *Women and Leadership: The State of Play and Strategies for Change.* San Francisco: Jossey Bass.

Khan, M. 2005. Moderate Muslims Are the Key to the Future of Islam and American Muslim Relations. *American Journal of Islamic Social Sciences* 22 (3): 72–75.

Knapp, J. C. 2007. *For the Common Good: The Ethics of Leadership in the 21st Century.* Westport, CT: Praeger Publishers.

Ko, D., K. Haboush, and J. Piggot. 2003. *Women and Confucian Cultures in Premodern China, Korea, and Japan.* Berkeley: University of California Press.

Koh, W., R. Steers, and J. Terborg. 1996. An Empirical Validation of the Theory of Transformational Leadership in Secondary Schools in Singapore. *Journal of Organisational Behaviour* 16 (4): 319–333.

Kolb, D., and K. McGuinn. 2009. Beyond Gender and Negotiations to Gendered Negotiations. *International Association for Conflict Management* 2 (1): 1–16.

Komives, S. 2005. Religion, Spirituality and Leadership. *Journal of College and Character* 6 (5) Article 11.

Korac-Kakabadse, N., A. Kouzmin, and A. Kakabadse. 2002. Spirituality and Leadership Praxis. *Journal of Managerial Psychology* 17 (3): 165–182.

Kouzes, J. M., and B. Z. Posner. 2002. *Leadership Challenge.* 3d ed. San Francisco: Jossey Bass.

Krishnakumar, S., and C. Neck. 2002. The "What," "Why," and "How" of Spirituality in the Workplace. *Journal of Managerial Psychology* 17 (3):153–164.

Kristoff, N. 2011. Democracy in the Brotherhood's Birthplace. *New York Times,* December 10. Retrieved on December 12, 2011, from http://www.nytimes.com/2011/12/11/opinion/sunday/kristof-Democracy-in-the-Muslim-Brotherhoods-Birthplace.html?_r=0.

Larson, C. L. 1997. Representing the Subject: Problems in Personal Narrative Inquiry. *International Journal of Qualitative Studies in Education* 10 (4): 455–470.

Lebra, T. S. 1998. Confucian Gender Roles and Personal Fulfilment for Japanese Women. In *Confucianism and the Family,* edited by G. De Vos and W. Slote, 209–224. New York: State University of New York Press.

Li, I., L. Wang, and K. W. Fischer. 2003. The Organization of Shame Concepts in Chinese. *Cognitive Development Laboratory Report.* Cambridge, MA: Harvard University.

Lifschultz, L., and K. Bird. 1979. Bangladesh: Anatomy of a Coup. *Economic and Political Weekly* 14 (49): 1999–2014.

Lin, C. 2008. Demystifying the Chameleonic Nature of Chinese Leadership. *Journal of Leadership and Organisational Studies* 14 (4): 303–321.

Lips-Wiersma, M., and C. Mills. 2002. Coming out of the Closet: Negotiating Spiritual Expression in the Workplace. *Journal of Managerial Psychology* 17 (3): 183–202.

Liu, Y., J. Liu, and L. Wu. 2010. Are You Willing and Able? Roles of Motivation, Power, and Politics in Career Growth. *Journal of Management* 36 (6): 1432–1460.

Lombardo, M. M., and R. W. Eichinger. 2006. *The Leadership Machine.* Greensboro, NC: Lominge.

Luce, E. 2007. *In Spite of the Gods: The Strange Rise of Modern India.* New York: Doubleday.

Maalouf, A. (1996) 2001. *In the Name of Identity: Violence and the Need to Belong.* New York: Grasset and Fasquelle.

Madgavkar, A. 2012. *India's Missing Women Workforce.* McKinsey Global Institute. http://www.mckinsey.com/insights/mgi/in_the_news/india_missing_women _workforce

Manji, I. 2003. *The Trouble with Islam: A Muslim's Call for Reform in Her Faith.* New York: St Martins Press.

Matsui, K., H. Sizuki, C. Eoyang, T. Akiba, and K. Tatebe. 2010. *Japan: Portfolio Strategy. Womenonics 3.0: The Time is Now.* Goldman Sachs Research, 1–37.

Mattson, I. 2005. Can a Woman be an Imam? Debating Form and Function in Muslim Women's Leadership Sisters. In *Women, Religion, and Leadership in Christianity and Islam,* edited by S. Alexander, 1–21. London: Sheed and Ward.

McCall, M. 1998. *High Flyers: Developing the Next Generation of Leaders.* Boston, MA: Harvard Business School Press.

McCaughan, D. 2012. The Truth about Asian Women. McCann Truth Central, http://truthcentral.mccann.com/.

McGonigal, J. 2011. *Reality is Broken: Why Games Make Us Better and How They can Change the World.* New York: Penguin Press.

McKee, A., F. Johnston, and R. Massimilian. 2006. Mindfulness, Hope, and Compassion: A Leader's Road Map to Renewal. *Ivey Business Journal,* May–June, 1–6.

McNeil, M. 2010. Alternate Approaches to Reaching Women: Engaging With Muslim Women Reformers. *St. Francis Magazine: Interserve and Arab Vision* 6 (5): 797–820.

References

Miller, T. 2012. *China's Urban Billion: The Story Behind the Biggest Migration in Human History.* New York: Zed Books.

Mintzberg, H. (1989) 2007. *Mintzberg on Management: Inside Our Strange World of Organizations.* New York, NY: Free Press.

Merchant, K. 2012. How Men And Women Differ: Gender Differences in Communication Styles, Influence Tactics, and Leadership Styles. *CMC Senior Theses.* Paper 513, http://scholarship.claremont.edu/cmc_theses/513.

Mitchell, C. 2012. A Narrative Inquiry of Women's Lives in Mugu, Nepal: Identities, Power Relations, and Education. PhD diss., Queens University, Belfast.

Moen, D. 1992. Emergent Culture of Japanese Organic Farming: Miyoshi Producer Group–Tokyo Consumer Group Co-Partnership. *Journal of Social Science (Japan)* 31 (2): 80–115.

Moen, D. 1997. The Japanese Organic Farming Movement: Consumers and Farmers United. *Bulletin of Concerned Asian Scholars* 29 (4): 60–73.

Montouri, A. 2010. Transformative Leadership for the Twenty-First Century: Reflections on the Design of a Graduate Leadership Curriculum. *ReVision* 30 (3 and 4): 4–14.

Montouri, A. 2013. Complexity and Transdisciplinarity: Reflections on Theory and Practice. *World Futures: The Journal of Education* 69 (4–6): 200–230.

Morgan, G. 1997. *Images of Organization.* Thousand Oaks, CA: Sage.

Mydans, S. 2007 Across Cultures English is the Word. *New York Times,* April, http://www.nytimes.com/2007/04/09/world/asia/09iht-englede.1.5198685.html?pagewanted=all.

Nadoff, Tricia. 2005. Leading Authentically: New Research into the Link between Essential Self and Leadership Effectiveness. In *Enlightened Power: How Women are Transforming the Practice of Leadership,* edited by Lyn Couglin, Ellen Wingard, and Ektih Holihan, 301–314. San Francisco, CA: Jossey-Bass.

Oberman, R., R. Dobbs, A. Budiman, F. Thomson, and M. Rosse. 2012. The Archipelago Economy: Unleashing Indonesia's Potential. *McKinsey Quarterly,* 1–116.

Ong, A. 1995. Women Out of China: Travelling Tales and Travelling Theories in Postcolonial Feminism. In *Women Writing Culture,* edited by R. Behar and D. Gordon, 351–372. Los Angeles: University of California Press.

Parker-Pope, T. 2010. As Girls Become Women, Sports Pay Dividends. *New York Times,* February, 16. Retrieved on March 04, 2011, from http://well.blogs.nytimes.com/2010/02/15/as-girls-bcome-women-sports-pay-dividencd/.

Pellows, D. 1993. Chinese Privacy. In *The Cultural Meaning of Urban Space,* edited by R. Rotenberg and G. McDonough, 32–33. New York: Praeger.

Petererson, C., and M. Seligman. 2004. *Characters, Strengths, and Virtues: A Handbook and Classification.* Oxford, UK: Oxford University Press.

Perrewe, P., and D. Nelson. 2004. The Facilitative Role of Political Skill. *Organisational Dynamics* 33 (4): 366–378.

Peshkova, S. 2009. Muslim Women Leaders in Ferghana Valley: Whose Leadership Is It Anyway? *Journal of International Women's Studies* 11 (1): 5–24.

Phillion, J. 2002. Becoming a Narrative Inquirer in a Multicultural Landscape. *Journal of Curriculum Studies* 34 (5): 535–556.

Pickles, J., and J. Woods. 1989. Taiwan Investment in South Africa. *African Affairs* 88 (353): 507–528.

Pink, D. 2006. *A Whole New Mind: Why Right-Brainers Will Rule the Future.* New York: Riverhead Books.

Pinnegar, S., and J. G. Daynes. 2000. Locating Narrative Inquiries Historically. In *Handbook of Narrative Inquiry: Mapping a Methodology,* edited by D. J. Clandinin, 3–33. Thousand Oaks, CA: Sage.

Polkinghorne, D. 1995. Narrative Configuration in Qualitative Analysis. *International Journal of Qualitative Studies in Education* 8 (1): 6–23.

Pollock, D., and R. Van Reken. 1999. *The Third Culture Kid Experience: Growing Up among Worlds.* Maine: Intercultural Press.

Probyn, E. 1996. *Outside Belongings.* New York: Routledge.

Rashid, S. F. 2006. Small Powers, Little Choice: Contextualising Reproductive and Sexual Rights in the Slums of Bangladesh. *Institute of Development Bulletin* 37 (5): 69–76.

Rashiduzzaman, M. 1994. The Liberals and the Religious Right in Bangladesh. *Asian Survey* 34 (11): 974–990.

Ray, R., and D. Learmond. 2013. DNA of Leaders. *Leadership Development Secrets Conference Board Research Report.*

Ray, R., J. Gornick, and J. Schmidtt. 2009. *Parental Leave Policies in 21 Countries: Assessing Generosity and Gender Equality,* 1–25. Washington, DC: Center for Economic and Policy Research (CEPR).

Reinharz, S. 1992. *Feminist Methods in Social Research.* New York: Oxford University Press.

Reinharz, S., and S. Chase. 2001. Interviewing Women. In *Handbook of Interview Research: Context and Method,* edited by J. Gubrium and J. Holstein, 221–238. Thousand Oaks, CA: Sage.

Rhode, D. 2003. *The Difference "Difference" Makes: Women and Leadership.* Stanford CA: Stanford University Press.

Richardson, L., 1994. Writing: A Method of Inquiry In *Handbook of Qualitative Research,* edited by N. K. Denzin and Y. S. Lincoln, 516–529. Thousand Oaks, CA: Sage.

Richardson, L., and E. St. Pierre. 2005. Writing: A Method of Inquiry. In *The Handbook of Qualitative Research,* 3d ed., edited by Norman K. Denzin and Yvonne S. Lincoln, 959–978. London: Sage.

Richman, J. 2011. Hillary Clinton Calls on Asia-Pacific Nations to Empower Women for Global Economic Growth. *Oakland Tribune,* September 16.

Ridgeway, C. L. 2011. *Framed by Gender: How Gender Inequality Persists in the Modern World.* London: Oxford University Press.

Riessman, C. K. 1993. *Narrative Analysis.* Newbury Park, CA: Sage.

Riessman, C. K. 2000. Analysis of Personal Narratives. In *Handbook of Qualitative Research,* edited by N. K. Denzin and Y. S. Lincoln, 695–710. Thousand Oaks, CA: Sage.

Riessman, C. K. 2008. *Narrative Methods for the Human Science.* London UK: Sage Publications.

Rosener, J. 1990. Ways Women Lead. *Harvard Business Review.* November /December.

Rosin, H. 2012. *The End of Men and the Rise of Women.* London: Penguin Press.

Ross, H. 2008. Exploring Unconscious Bias. Diversity Best Practice Report. *CDO Insights* 2 (5): 1–18.

Russell, B. 1975. *Autobiography of Bertrand Russell.* New York: Routledge.

Safi, L. 2005. Reflections on *Ijtihad,* Moderate Islam. *American Journal of Islamic Social Sciences* 22 (3): 91–94.

Sandberg, S. 2013. *Lean In: Women, Work, and the Will to Lead.* New York, NY: Knopf.

Sandel, M. J. 2007. *Justice: A Reader.* Oxford: Oxford University Press.

Sankhe, S., I. Vittal, R. Dobbs, A. Mohan, J. Ablett, S. Gupta, et al. 2010. India's Urban Awakening: Building Inclusive Cities and Sustaining Economic Growth. *McKinsey Global Institute,* 1–234.

Sarup, M., and T. Raja. 1996. *Identity, Culture, and the Postmodern World.* Edinburgh: Edinburgh University Press.

Shope, J. 2006. You Can't Cross A River Without Getting Wet: A Feminist Standpoint on the Dilemmas of Cross-Cultural Research. *Qualitative Inquiry* 12 (1): 163–184.

Silverstein, M., and K. Sayer. 2009. The Female Economy. *Harvard Business Review,* September, 1–8.

Skeggs, B. 2001. Feminist Ethnography. In *Handbook of Ethnography,* edited by P. Atkinson, A. Coffee, S. Delamont, J. Lofland, and L. Lofland, 11–25. London: Sage Publications.

Solomon, R. 2004. Ethical Leadership, Emotions, and Trust: Beyond "Charisma." In *Ethics: The Heart of Leadership,* edited by Joanne Ciulla, 83–102. Westport, CT: Praeger.

Sparkes, A. C. 2002. *Telling Tales in Sports and Physical Activity: A Qualitative Journey.* London: Human Kinetics.

Speedy, J. 2008. *Narrative Inquiry and Psychotherapy.* Hampshire: Palgrave Macmillan.

Spence, J. 1990. *The Search for Modern China.* New York: Norton.

Spindler, J. 2008. Fictional Writing, Educational Research, and Professional Learning. *International Journal of Research and Method in Education* 31 (1): 19–30.

Stivers, C. 1993. Reflections on the Role of Personal Narrative. *Social Science Review* 18 (2): 408–425.

Sultana, A. M., J. Jawan, and I. Hashim. 2009. The Influence of *Purdah* (Veil) on Education and Employment in Rural Communities. *European Journal of Social Sciences* 11 (2): 267–280.

Swenson, D. 2009. *Society, Spirituality, and the Scared: A Social Scientific Introduction.* 2d ed. Ontario: University of Toronto Press.

Talukder, M. 1975. Bangladesh: An Unfinished Revolution? *Journal of Asian Studies* 34 (4): 891–911.

Tannen, D. 2001. *You Just Don't Understand: Men and Women in Conversation*. New York: Harper-Collins.

Tannen, D. (1994) 2013. *Talking from 9 to 5: Men and Women at Work*. New York: Harper-Collins.

Tarr-Whelan, L. 2009. *Women Lead The Way: Your Guide to Stepping Up to Leadership and Changing the World*. San Francisco: Berrett-Koehler.

Taylor, P., and S. Keeter. 2010. Milennials: A Portrait of Generation Next. Confident. Connected and Open to Change. *Pew Research Center*, February, 1–113.

Thomas, R., J. Tiernari, A. Davies, and S. Merilainen. 2009. Let's Talk about "Us": A Reflexive Account of a Cross-Cultural Research Collaboration Act. *Journal of Management Inquiry* 18 (4): 313–324.

Thompson, M. D. 2000. Gender, Leadership Orientation, and Effectiveness: Testing the Theoretical Models of Bolman, Deal, and Quinn. *Sex Roles* 42 (11/12): 969–992.

Thompson, M. R. 2002–2003. Female Leadership of Democratic Transitions in Asia. *Public Affairs* 75 (4): 535–555.

Tilly, C. 1996. *Citizenship, Harmony, and Social Harmony*. Cambridge, UK: Press Syndicate of the University of Cambridge.

Tilly, C. 1998. *Double Inequality*. Berkeley, CA: University of California Press.

Tilly, C. 2002. *Stories, Identities, and Political Change*. New York, NY: Rowan and Littlefield.

Tilly, C. 2005. *Identities, Boundaries, and Social Ties*. Boulder, CO: Paradigm.

Tilly, C. 2006. *Why?* New Jersey: Princeton University Press.

Tischler, L., J. Biberman, and R. McKeage. 2002. Linking Emotional Intelligence, Spirituality, and Workplace Performance: Definitions, Models, and Ideas for Research. *Journal of Managerial Psychology* 17 (3): 203–218.

Tolle, E. 1999. *The Power of Now: A Guide to Spiritual Enlightenment*. Novato, CA: New World Library.

Torres, I. 2013. Abe's Vow to Elevate Women in Japanese Society Being Undermined by Male-dominated Politics. *Japan Daily Press*, June 18, http://japandailypress.com/abes-vow-to-elevate-women-in-japanese-society-being-undermined-by-male-dominated-politics-1830752/.

Trahar, S. 2006. *Narrative Research on Learning: Comparative and International Perspectives*. Cambridge: Cambridge University Press.

Trahar, S. 2009. Beyond the Story Itself: Narrative Inquiry and Autoethnography in Intercultural Research in Higher Education. *Forum: Qualitative Social Research* 10 (1): 30. Retrieved January 15, 2011, from http://www.qualitative-research.net/index.php/fqs/article/viewArticle/1218/2653.

Trahar, S. 2011. *Learning and Teaching Narrative Inquiry: Travelling into the Borderlands*. Amsterdam: John Benjamin Publishing.

Trompenaars, F. 1997. *Riding the Waves of Culture: Understanding Cultural Diversity in Business*. London: Nicholas Brealey.

Tuminez, A. 2012. *Rising to the Top? A Report on Women's Leadership in Asia*. Singapore: Lee Kuan Yew School of Public Policy, National University of Singapore.

Vickers-Willis, R. 2002. *Navigating Midlife: Women Becoming Themselves.* Crows Nest, AU: Allen and Unwin.

Visweswaran, K. 1994. *Fictions of Feminist Ethnography.* Minneapolis: University of Minnesota Press.

Waldman, K. 2012. In Defence of Sheryl Sandberg. *Slate.* Retrieved on February 7, 2012. from http://www.slate.com/blogs/xx_factor/2012/02/07/sheryl_sandberg_is_right_about_the_ambition_gap_for_women_.html.

Walker, D. 2011. Private Companies Aren't Always a Beacon for the Public Sector. *The Guardian,* April 18.

Wang, B., and H. Chee. 2011. *Chinese Leadership.* London: Palgrave MacMillan.

Wang, J., G. Wang, W. Ruona, and J. Rojewski. 2005. Confucian Values and Implications for HRD. *Human Resource Development International* 8 (3): 311–326.

Wilson, M. C. 2007. *Closing the Leadership Gap: Add Women, Change Everything.* New York: Penguin Press.

Winfield, B. H., T. Mizuno, and C. E. Beaudoin. 2000. Confucianism, Collectivism, and Constitutions: Press Systems in China and Japan. *Communications Law and Policy* 5 (3): 323–347.

Wingard, E. 2005. Cultivating Still Point: The Power of Reflective Leadership. In *Enlightened Power: How Women are Transforming the Practice of Leadership,* edited by Lyn Couglin, Ellen Wingard, and Ektih Holihan, 169–194. San Francisco, CA: Jossey-Bass.

Wong, J. K. 2004. Are the Learning Styles of Asian International Students Culturally or Contextually Based? *International Education Journal Educational Research Conference 2003 Special Issue* 4 (4): 154–166.

Yoder, J. 2001. Making Leadership Work Effective for Women. *Journal of Social Science* 57 (4): 815–828.

Yuan, B., and S. Church, eds. 2000. *Oxford Starter Chinese Dictionary.* New York: Oxford University Press.

Chinese Online Dictionaries:

http://www.tigernt.com/cgi-bin/ecdict.cgi.

http://translate.google.com/and#x0023;zh-CNand#x007C;zh-CNand#x007C; Failure.

http://www.springerlink.com/content/n6221m42p450plh5/.

INDEX